Like a Dream

My Life Serving God

by

Edilberto "Bert" Colosaga

Like a Dream
Copyright © 2026—Edilberto Consigna Colosaga
ALL RIGHTS RESERVED

Unless otherwise noted, all Scripture references are from the *Holy Bible, King James Version*. References marked "NIV" are from the *Holy Bible, New International Version,* copyright © 1973, 1978, 1984 by International Bible Society, Colorado Springs, Colorado. References marked "TLB" are from *The Living Bible* paraphrased by Kenneth Taylor, copyright © 1971 by Tyndale House Publishers, Inc., Wheaton, Illinois. References marked "NKJV" are from *The Holy Bible, New King James Version*, copyright © 1979, 1980, 1982, 1990 by Thomas Nelson, Inc., Nashville, Tennessee. References marked "NOG" are from *The Names of God Bible,* copyright © 2011 by Baker Publishing Group, Ada, Michigan. References marked "GNT" are from *The Holy Bible, Good News Translation,* copyright © 1992 by The American Bible Society, New York, NY. Used by permission. All rights reserved.

Published by:

McDougal Publishing
www.mcdougalpublishing.com

ISBN: 978-1-58158-217-8

Printed on demand in the U.S., the U.K., and Australia
For Worldwide Distribution

As His divine power has given to us all things that pertain to life and godliness, through the knowledge of Him who called us by glory and virtue, by which have been given to us exceedingly great and precious promises, that through these you may be partakers of the divine nature, having escaped the corruption that is in the world through lust.
—2 Peter 1:3-4, NKJV

Dedication

To **Emilio B. Colosaga**, my father, a spiritual pillar in our local church and in the Colosaga family, who prayed for us constantly and sent encouraging letters when we were so far away in Ecuador.

To **Teresita B. Colosaga**, whose conversion led to our family becoming Christians, having a personal relationship with Christ, and later into studying God's Word and growing spiritually.

Contents

Introduction 9

1. Off to Bible School 11
2. A Special Touch from God 14
3. God's Hand on My Family 16
4. The Coming of the Holy Spirit 18
5. The Move to Tanay, Rizal 22
6. My Teaching Ministry Officially Begins 24
7. Typhoon Yoling: A Disaster or a Blessing in Disguise? 25
8. Everything Moves to Quezon City 27
9. The Spiritual Fiesta Crusades 31
10. Striking Gold 34
11. Part of the First CTTP Teams To Go Abroad 38
12. Wedding Bells 41
13. Into the Fire in Vietnam 44
14. How Would Marshal Law Affect Us? 48
15. Walking Where Jesus Walked 50
16. Arriving in the U.S. 51
17. Visiting the Camp in Ashland, Virginia 54
18. An Unexpected Gift from God 56
19. The Amazing Miracles of Ecuador 58
20. New Life Camp Activities 62

21. Reaching Out to the Nations 66
22. Back in the Philippines 69
23. Getting Back to Work 71
24. The Miracles of Those Years 73
25. The Seeds of Worship and Praise Missionary Training Center .. 76
26. A Battle for the Vision 80
27. Fruit That Remains 83
28. Meeting the Ridenours 85
29. The Walking Bible 88
30. The Korean Connection 90
31. Dealing with the Unlucky Number 13 92
32. Beulah Louise 95
33. The Miracle of Hannah 97
34. Our Trip to Vietnam, Cambodia, and Thailand 99
35. Sister Peggy's Contribution 103
36. Fruit in Vietnam 105
37. My Premonitions 107

MESSAGES:

The Lord Is My Shepherd 112
The Gospel According to Isaiah 53 124
Essentials for Growth and the Building Up of the Body of Christ 130
2 TIMOTHY 1
    DISCIPLESHIP—PRINCIPLES AND MOBILIZATIONS 134
2 TIMOTHY 2
    DISCIPLE MAKERS: CHARACTERISTICS 137

2 TIMOTHY 3
    DISCIPLESHIP- SUSTAINABILITY AMIDST CRISES............ 141
2 TIMOTHY 4
    DISCIPLESHIP—COMMISSIONING AND LAUNCHING ... 144
JAMES 1
    TRIED AND TESTED 147
JAMES 2
    WHAT'S WRONG WITH DISCRIMINATION? 151
JAMES 3
    TAMING THE TONGUE 155
JAMES 4
    PRAYING OR PREYING 159
JAMES 5
    WHAT ARE WE LIVING FOR? 163

Introduction

I was standing before several hundred young people in a beautiful Andean scene, a tent erected beside a lake in a beautiful camp in Ecuador. I was sharing the Good News of the Gospel with young people who had gathered from several South American nations. They were so hungry for God that the atmosphere was charged that night, and I sensed a special anointing upon me and upon the words I was speaking.

When the altar call was given, the crowd surged forward to eagerly receive Christ, and when I invited them all to pray to receive the baptism of the Holy Spirit, the response was so remarkable that it took many coworkers to help me lay hands on and pray for all those who responded. It was an Andean Pentecost.

In one way, it was all like a dream. How could a humble Filipino from the small town of Lal-lo in Northern Luzon reach such heights? It was inconceivable that at such a young age I had already been to many nations. Surely it was all because of the Lord's blessing and favor upon my life, and all the glory was unto Him. This is my story.

Bert Colosaga
Parañaque, Metro Manila, Philippines

Off to Bible School

In 1966, I went to Bible school at Anchor Bay Bible Institute in my home province of Cagayan. I had originally enrolled in Manuel L. Quezon University in Metro Manila but had then transferred to Cagayan Teachers' College in Tuguegarao. This was all part of God's way of confirming His calling upon my life, and it happened in the following way.

After high school, I came to Manila to pursue college. My aunt, who was a teacher in a high school, suggested that I pursue a Bachelor of Arts degree, as this would open me up to whatever work I chose to do in the future, maybe in law or medicine. The reason I came to Manila was that my elder sister was studying here to be a teacher, and my youngest aunt was also finishing her high school in Manila.

But the circumstances soon changed. After one year in college, my sister decided to get married, and my aunt answered the call to ministry and wanted to go to Bible school. This meant if I wanted to continue studying in Manila that next year, I would have to make the long trip to Manila with my grandmother. She would serve as chaperone and cook for me and wash my clothes. That was the arrangement made by my parents, but it was not very convenient for me. It required adjusting to a totally new setup and moving to a new boarding house. I would no longer be with friends and relatives as before.

I also had problems with the transportation to and from Manila. It was a twenty-hour bus trip, plus three jeepney rides. As the next semester approached, my father decided it would be easier on the family financially if I transferred to the province. As much as I wanted to continue studying in Manila, it was becoming nearly impossible because of the distance. Considering the suggestion of my father regarding his support for my college, that semester I had to pack my things and head back north.

This move seemed demeaning to me. People considered the level of education to be far superior in Manila, so now I had to humble myself and accept this demotion of status. It also seemed disruptive in other ways. Moving to Manila had been exciting. Now, I seemed to be constantly asking, "Lord, what do You want me to do now?" Was I not finding God's will for my life?

Added to the burden of travel with my eighty-year-old grandmother, a storm arose, a serious storm, a typhoon that destroyed one of the bridges we would need to cross. Nature didn't seem to be cooperating and was making it harder to travel.

Because that bridge was destroyed, we had to transfer to a boat. The problem was we had come with many pieces of luggage. Now I had to transfer all of that luggage from the bus to the boat. The pathway was downhill, and it was raining and very slippery. It seemed like a very round-about way to get back home, but there was no other way. The trip this time took twenty-four hours. Maybe studying in the province was better after all.

2

A Special Touch from God

That next semester I enrolled at CTC, and life there seemed rather mundane and uneventful. But God had a plan.

Because I was staying in Tuguegarao, only a few hours by bus from my hometown of Lal-lo, it was easier for me to attend church services at home on Sundays, and I did that. During one Sunday service, Evangelist Cornelio Saboya was our invited speaker. He was very anointed as he delivered God's Word, and after preaching he called for anyone who would like to receive prayer to come forward. I immediately responded, for I sensed that I needed more of God.

As I went to the front, I felt a strong presence of the Lord. Brother Saboya laid hands on everyone who had come forward and prayed for us. When he prayed for me, I went down in the power of the Holy Spirit and lay there feeling the Spirit's strong presence washing over me.

A Special Touch from God

That afternoon I went back to school, as the semester was not yet finished. I sensed that something had changed dramatically with me. The following day I was alone in my dormitory room when I again felt God's presence, and I wept uncontrollably. As I waited on the Lord that day, I heard His soft voice calling me to serve Him, calling me to give Him my life, calling me to share the Good News, the Gospel, with others in need. This was such a radical commitment that I did a lot of praying to make sure I had heard God correctly, and I would need firm confirmations of this calling.

I decided to ask my father to allow me to go to Bible school the next school year, and I asked God to let my father say yes as a sign that I was on the right track.

God's Hand on My Family

My father was himself a pillar of the church, having become a preacher and Sunday school teacher after surrendering to Jesus Christ and receiving Him as Lord and Savior. This came about because my aunt, before finishing her college studies in Manila, came to know Christ in a church here in the city. She, her younger sister, and my oldest sister all three became Christians here in Manila and soon began to reach out to the rest of the family, sharing God's Word with the rest of us. Before long, more of us felt our need of the Lord, and my father became a committed Christian.

Very quickly my father became a man of serious prayer. He prayed morning and evening. He would take a small kerosene lamp and cross our street to the church where he would pray. Being the eldest of nine children, he prayed for the whole family, and God was soon at work in the whole family, In time, most of the members who eventually made up the church in Lal-lo were my relatives. God answered my father's prayers, and many in the family became leaders in the church.

After consulting with my mother and the rest of the family, Tatang decided to donate a portion of our land, some 200 square meters, for a church building. Over the years, the resulting building went from a simple bamboo edifice to a lovely all-concrete structure. Much of this was thanks to the initiative of my youngest brother. He, along with the elders and other church members, made many improvements.

Three years before I made my decision to serve God, my Aunt Isabel had also made a decision to go to Bible school and serve the Lord. Somehow her calling gave me the encouragement I needed to make the same move. I finally got up my courage to ask my dad's permission to go to the Bible school. At first, he seemed hesitant. Then his answer was, "Well, you can try it." He seemed to be saying that if I ever changed my mind, I would be welcome to pursue another course. Thankfully, changing course never crossed my mind. Once I was on this pathway, there was no turning back. Serving God was the best decision I could have ever made, and I never regretted it.

4

The Coming of the Holy Spirit

In 1967, as I went about the daily routine of prayers, devotions, and Bible readings in the Bible School, I became desperately hungry for how others moved in the Holy Spirit, how they were able to pray in the Spirit, speaking in tongues. I can never forget what happened on Friday, July 7, 1967.

In our prayer room that morning, the Holy Spirit came upon me, and I began to speak in other tongues. There are no words to adequately describe what I felt in those moments. I sensed that I was touching God in a new way, and my prayer in the Spirit continued for about an hour. The other students had left, but I was reluctant to stop praying in this wonderful way.

Even after I had moved on to our dorm and to the rest of the daily routine, the Lord's presence was with me. I couldn't help but give thanks for this, another strong confirmation of my calling.

Another strong confirmation came when the semester was over and I went back home for vacation. That Wednesday night, at the regular prayer meeting, the pastor asked me if I would preach. At first I hesitated because I had never preached before, and this would be my first experience at sharing the Word of God. He insisted. Fortunately, the Lord dropped 2 Chronicles 7:14 into my spirit and I read it:

"If my people who are called by my name shall humble themselves and pray and seek my face and turn from their wicked ways, then will I hear from heaven. I will forgive their sins and heal their lands."

As I stood and read those words, an amazing thing happened. I felt a great anointing, and other words began flowing from my mouth. I was so moved by this experience that I began to weep, and then the congregation began to weep too.

I didn't know what to do next, but I said to the people, "Let it flow! Just let it flow!" And we all stood in God's presence and let the Spirit flow. I never forgot it. It was my first time to preach, and yet God had moved so wonderfully.

Like a Dream

Back at the Bible school, aside from the usual theology subjects and other important subjects related to the course I was taking, we had a weekly program of outreach to a nearby village, a Barrio of Santa Marcela of the Province of Apayao. In later years, Christ to the Philippines would established some nine growing churches in that province. Each Saturday we preached to the families and neighbors of one of our fellow students.

When it came time for summer break, I asked to be allowed to partner with Ben, a more mature brother, soon to graduate and become a pastor. A few years ago, I learned that Ben is now the President of the entire Haven of Rest organization.

The church Ben and I ministered to that summer was in a remote village in the Sierra Madre Mountains. I have never forgotten that summer—doing evangelism and conducting children's ministry and house prayer meetings. It was two months of wonderful practical ministry experience that helped prepare me for what was ahead. Too soon the summer ended, and for the ten members of that fourth-year class, it was graduation time. Our missionaries, the Marsacks, invited a young American missionary named Harold McDougal as speaker that year, and he came with

The Coming of the Holy Spirit

another young American, Calvin Lawson. I was not able to meet Brother Harold personally at that time, but it was a blessing to hear the Word of God from this servant.

5

The Move to Tanay, Rizal

Unbeknownst to us students, an arrangement was reached between the two missionary groups to join forces and merge our Anchor Bay Bible Institute with a Bible school the McDougals were putting up in Sampaloc, Tanay, Rizal, a few hours outside of Manila. And so, by June of 1968, most of the school staff and all the students, second and third year, moved to Sampaloc. I recall traveling from Lal-lo, Cagayan with two others to 108 Kapok Street in Caloocan City, the address we had been given.

After we arrived there, the McDougals asked Sister Peggy Boutchyard, another of the young missionaries, to escort us up to the Bible School. After a jeepney ride and two more bus rides, we finally arrived at the place. Some of our fellow students from Cagayan had already arrived ahead of us.

The site was still in its pioneering stages and, until then, had been only used by the missionaries for their summer campmeeting programs. The land had been donated by the Sanoy family for religious purposes, and two crude dormitories had been constructed, one for the girls and another for the boys. The staff housing was also made of very light materials, as was the open-air dining room that also served as an assembly area. The beds were made of bamboo, which was easy to harvest nearby at the time.

The only source of water was so far away that a tank was used for drinking and cooking water. It was filled three times a week by a truck coming from the barrio center. For bathing and clothes washing, we had to walk some 500 meters to a small stream. It was a pleasant place to bathe … unless the carabaos got there first. Eventually a well was drilled on the lower part of the property, and the water problem was solved. But that was in years to come.

Aside from our studies, we students did outreach ministry in the nearby villages of Sampaloc, Balimbing, Tanay, Baras, and Pililla.

By 1969, a new building was put up along with a mission house. Students came from the towns of Rizal, from the Ilongot tribes of Quezon Province, and from the Ilocano speaking provinces.

6

My Teaching Ministry Officially Begins

When I finished my first year in that school, I had the feeling that I would be assigned to pastor in one of the churches in my home province of Cagayan, but God had other plans. The principal of the school, Alfredo Domingo, tapped me to teach that next year. It was my first year for teaching, and aside from the Ilocano students, there were now students from Quezon Province, Rizal, Bulacan, and Nueva Ecija.

The following year brought an even larger group. These were from Surigao and the Visayas, particularly from the island of Gibusong, as a result of the missionaries' visit to that island. That year, we had to divide classes into English, Tagalog, and Ilocano, depending on which language the students understood best. I had to teach classes in all three languages.

7

Typhoon Yoling: A Disaster or a Blessing in Disguise?

In November of that year, Typhoon Yoling hit the area. It was an unforgettable experience for me. I and another brother were on the upper floor of the two-story building when an especially strong gust of wind ripped off the roof, and much of that second floor came crashing down. We suddenly found ourselves outside on a pile of collapsed concrete blocks. The other brother suffered a broken wrist, and I lost two front teeth, but we were otherwise unhurt and glad to be alive.

The sharp metal roofing sections that had blown off had missed us by mere inches. The rest of the students and staff had already evacuated to the ground floor of the missionary house, but that roof was also blown off, and the ground floor walls had collapsed. Still, all of them were safe.

When the missionaries in Caloocan City learned about what had happened and came to get us, they

Like a Dream

found that not a single structure was left standing on their way from Tanay to Sampaloc. Yoling had destroyed them all. We were all safe, but our belongings, including our clothes, were lost. All we had left was what we had on.

We were all taken to the Murphy Church, students and staff and their families. The problem was that the storm had also affected that area, and many neighbors who had lost their homes were also being housed in the church. The building was packed with people fleeing the wrath of the storm, and we had to find a spot to sit and to sleep. It is believed by many that this strange combination of students, teachers, neighbors, and missionaries—all thrown together in that cramped space—is what gave rise to the revival that soon followed.

8

Everything Moves to Quezon City

As soon as the space could be found, we continued to have classes and times of prayer. It was decided that the Bible school should be kept in Murphy, and two nearby apartments were rented, one to house the men and the other to house the women.

Eventually a deserted theater housed in a Quonset hut on 13th Avenue was leased for this purpose. It was a very large building, and accommodated everyone—students and some teachers and staff. There were boys' and girls' dorms, a kitchen and a dining room. Certain rooms were designated for married couples, and one room was given to Remy Fernandez, a widow, wife of a pastor, who served as school Matron and cook for everyone, and her daughter Mercy. Classes and services were conducted in the church, just a short walk away.

After the Spiritual Fiesta (about which I will relate more in the next chapter), with the revival spirit awash in the nation, the emphasis changed in the Bible school, and it became a missionary training center.

The year following the Spiritual Fiesta crusades, we had even more students. After graduation, these students were divided into teams and sent out to different schools in the area. The Minister of Education had provided a letter giving CTTP access to classrooms everywhere.

In each classroom, we sang, gave testimonies, preached a short message, prayed with the teachers and students, and then gave each one a printed gospel.

When we had covered in this way most of the schools in the Metro Manila area, each team was assigned to a certain province, and we repeated the same ministry there. In the process, we ministered to and distributed gospels of John to 1.2 million people, many of them students, the up-and-coming generation.

Aside from the teachers and students, our teams had several other areas of focus: ministry to any government officials in the area (especially mayors and governors), ministry to any military leaders in the area, and ministry to any religious leaders in the area (regardless of denomination). We carried with us books and Bible materials that were suitable to give to these leaders.

During the months the schools were not in session, our emphasis shifted. The Philippine Bible Society in Manila had a large stock of undistributed gospels in many tribal dialects, and we were able to secure these and take them to the unreached tribal areas. In this way, the teams assigned to these tribes had the privilege of giving the precious Word of God to many of the tribal people to read for the first time in their own dialect. I was privileged to lead a team to Abra, and Paz led a team to the Amganag tribes in Ifugao. Before it was over, we had covered all the major tribal groups in the country. This included Luzon, the Visayas, and Mindanao.

During this time of fruitful reaping, I was privileged to lead a team of four men to the island of Polillo, and also to Palawan and the islands of Cuyo.

Years later, we had a young man from Polillo, Jonathan Cañolas, who was very gifted in music and who enrolled in our Worship and Praise Missionary Center and studied with us for two years. After Jonathan graduated, I received a letter from Pastor Estelita Besas, who was serving the Namphrathai Church in Bangkok, Thailand, asking if we had any graduates who played music and could play for their worship services and also teach the musically inclined in her church how to play. Jonathan accepted this challenge and served there

Like a Dream

for two years. He was part of the 10th batch from our training center.

After serving for two years in Thailand, Jonathan went on to other areas. I believe he has now gone to New Zealand to teach music.

There were sometimes as many as ten CTTP teams out at once. Some of these teams were led by missionaries, but many were led by Filipinos. Our message was that Jesus is our Savior, Healer, and Baptizer in the Holy Spirit, the One who changes our lives. We also spoke of Him as our soon-coming King and urged people to be ready at all times. So many wonderful miracles resulted from all of this activity, and it all happened in just three short years.

The Spiritual Fiesta Crusades

The leaders of CTTP were led to conduct large outdoor crusades known as The Spiritual Fiesta. The first of these crusades was conducted in the Amoranto Stadium in Quezon City. This crusade was televised live, many physical healings were seen on live television, and this opened doors of ministry to many places—especially among Catholics.

After the Quezon City crusade, we travelled with a team to Iloilo City, then to Surigao City, and, lastly, to Naga City. These crusades brought many souls to the feet of Jesus, and many received healings and miracles in their bodies. This happened because there was unity among the group, whether it was in fasting, in praying, or in making sacrificial gifts. We all spent hours together in the presence of the Lord.

It was a time of great open doors. We suddenly had favor with many other Christian groups, especially Catholic priests and nuns, and this was taken advantage of with visits to their monasteries and nunneries.

Like a Dream

Many were filled with the Spirit. Especially receptive to our message were the Carmelite Sisters who gave themselves to prayer. Also new radio and television outreaches were established at this time.

Before the Manila-area crusade, large billboards were placed all around the city. These billboards proclaimed the biblical truth that God had given me during that first sermon:

> *If my people who are called by my name shall humble themselves and pray and seek my face and turn from their wicked ways, then will I hear from heaven. I will forgive their sins and heal their land.* 2 Chronicles 7:14

Years later, when many Filipinos came out to protest in the Edsa Revolution, at the corner of Edsa and Ortigas Avenues, this same verse was engraved in metal at the foot of a statue of Mary. It had become a powerful challenge to our nation.

Our Spiritual Fiesta team traveled to Iloilo City by ship. From there, we moved on, via another ship, to Surigao City. Then, after coming back to Manila by ship, we all traveled by train to Bicol and did the final crusade in Naga City. This one, like the first, was televised. It was all a life-changing experience.

I have often been asked what the secret was to the success of those early students of Tanay, Rizal and the Missionary Training Center in Murphy, faithful workers who have gone on to serve the Lord for many years as church leaders in many countries. There were, of course, many elements to that success. If I had to narrow it down to one, I would say it was because we were taught to live by faith, depending on God, and allowing Him to guide us and to provide everything we needed. This we did locally and also in foreign lands, as I will recount in coming chapters.

When we were assigned to a certain mission, whether inside or outside of our country, we were given a very limited amount of money and a ticket (sometimes one-way), but no contacts. We had to believe God to lead us and provide for us, and He never failed us. In this way, we developed a deep relationship with the Lord that carried us through every trial and test of life in the years to come.

10

Striking Gold

For quite a while now I had been very impressed with a certain young lady among the CTTP workers. She was Paz Degorio from the little island of Gibusong. Paz was an excellent person in every way. She was humble yet powerful. Her love of the Lord was evident to all, and she had shown excellent leadership in the teams she led. I began to think of her as the very best wife material any man could ever hope for and had been longing for some way to express my feelings to her and know her response. But there was a problem: one of the strict rules of the Bible school was that there was to be absolutely no courting allowed. How could I, as a teacher and team leader, break that rule? As we were traveling from Cebu to Surigao, I made a point of talking to Sunamita Degorio, Paz's sister. I asked her if Paz had a boyfriend, and she said no.

I decided to write Paz a letter, making her aware of my desires, and by the time we reached Naga I was able to get the letter to her. Inside the place where the ladies were housed, she read the letter and then hid it under her pillow. Somehow one of the girls found it and began telling everyone in the team about it. This upset Paz and she told the girl that if she wanted, she would give me to her.

When I heard about this, I knew that Paz had feelings for me, and I was hoping to receive a letter in return. By the time we got back to Murphy, however, there was no letter yet, and arrangements were being made to send us out in smaller teams to all parts of the Philippines. Paz and her team were sent to Zamboanga and parts of Mindanao, and I and my team were sent to Palawan.

Before the ship she and her team would take to Zamboanga left, I somehow learned the name of the ship and the day and scheduled time of its departure. I felt an urgency to talk to Paz in person about the letter. I took Roque, a student from Baguio, with me. He was my friend and was also close to Paz.

Fortunately for me, a storm was forecast to strike, and, because of it, the departure of the ship Paz was on had been delayed. I counted this a blessing in disguise. For me, this was a once-in-a-lifetime opportunity to find out if Paz felt the same way I did.

Despite the bad weather, Roque and I took the opportunity to visit Paz and her team. When we got there,

Like a Dream

I could see that she was happy to see me, and my heart leaped. In time, she and I were able to move to another part of the ship, where we could talk in private. It didn't take long to hear her positive answer, and I was the happiest man in the world.

Paz later told me that her trip to Mindanao had been joyous, and the ministry there had been the best ever. She, too, was walking on cloud nine.

After a time, all the teams assigned in Mindanao came together in Davao City for a wonderful Morris Cerullo Crusade. When her team got back to Manila, Paz and I began to make plans for our wedding. That year, I invited her, her sister Sunamita, and Rebecca Corea to accompany me and celebrate Christmas with my family in my hometown in Cagayan. I wanted Paz to meet my parents and relatives. During those days in Lal-lo, we would make more plans for the wedding.

It was an unforgettable experience for both of us, but especially for me, to sit beside Paz for the first time on the Pantranco bus crossing Luzon. The fact that we were stranded for several hours in Nueva Vizcaya because of a landslide didn't bother me at all. I was with the woman I loved and admired and wanted to marry.

I must have had some premonition about the delay we would occur because I had bought, for the first time in my life, two roasted chickens. When we encountered the landslide, there was nowhere to buy food. I was ready, and our needs were supplied. It was a wonderful trip, and Paz and I enjoyed getting to know each other better. My parents loved her too. I felt like I had struck gold.

Part of the First CTTP Teams To Go Abroad

Back in Murphy, plans were being made to send the first Filipino teams out to other countries. Several years before, when the first revelations came that led to the Spiritual Fiesta and its aftermath, one humble American sister, Ethel Marshpund, had seen a vision of fire going out in waves from the Philippines to all the surrounding nations, so prayer had been going up as to when and how this was to begin.

Our leaders felt it was time. God had shown them that teams should be sent to the nation to the north (Taiwan, officially known as the Republic of China) and the nation to south (Indonesia). I wasn't anticipating being sent out in these teams. My understanding was that it would be students, so I was pleasantly surprised when I was told that I would be included in the team to Indonesia. My teammate was Gani Coruña, and together we were to minister in Indonesia for the next two months.

Part of the First CTTP Teams To Go Abroad

One of our CTTP brothers had given Gani and me some leads in Indonesia, but these didn't bear much fruit. The way our CTTP teams usually got their leads, through prayer, proved to be the best way. We preached in Djakarta, Surabaya, and Malang—all on the island of Java. It was in Malang that we were received in a very special way, and the greater part of our time was, therefore, spent in that place. We stayed with a church there and worked with its leaders. Aside from ministering to their people, we also ministered in several schools and in several other churches. God moved so powerfully in one particular church, baptizing many with the Holy Spirit, that when it came time for us to leave, they didn't want us to go.

One Sunday, it was again my turn to deliver the message in a local church. I can't remember what the topic was that day, but while I was preaching, the Holy Spirit took control, and a great anointing flowed from on high. There were some tears of repentance, and then the members of the church began to weep, and so did everyone. The Spirit took control of the service. Feeling that move among the congregation was an awesome experience. God be glorified! We were learning just to let Him do what He wanted among us.

Like a Dream

We visited the island of Bali and spoke in one of the churches there. While in Malang, we met an elderly single man who was a devoted Christian and spoke good English. He was very helpful in making arrangements for meetings and even traveled with us to Jakarta when we were flying back home.

Paz had been chosen to lead the CTTP team to Taiwan. Her team members were Sunamita (her sister), Aida Padul (her niece), and Emma Querubin, a pastor's daughter. Their reports were amazing. In fact, their trip to Taiwan, I believe, resulted in what we reaped twenty years later when a team of Taiwanese believers led by Pastor Abel Yeh came to the Philippines and formed a partnership with us to build and manage the Worship and Praise Missionary Training Center in Parañaque. I will elaborate on that later in the book.

12

Wedding Bells

After we got back from our trips abroad, Paz and I got serious about making wedding plans. The date was set for June of 1972. It seemed fitting, at that moment, that all along we had been taught to live by faith, for neither of us had any money. Faith was all we had, but that was enough.

I was able to get together enough money to order new shoes and have a suit made, but that was all I could afford at the moment. I sent a telegram to my parents to please bring anything they could from the province, and they responded wonderfully, bringing crates full of chickens, sacks of rice, and whatever else was available.

Before the wedding, I needed to make the long journey to Gibusong, home of Paz, to meet her parents and other relatives and friends, and it was arranged. I also needed to provide the ship fares for her relatives coming that long distance to the wedding. These were the Madambas, the Degorios, and the Mahinays. God provided for my trip.

Like a Dream

Aida, Paz's niece, also a missionary of Christ to the Philippines, accompanied me to Gibusong. It was a trip of several days, made on ship and then smaller boats, and as we had to spend more and more, I wondered if I would have enough money left to still pay for everyone's round-trip passage to attend the wedding. I was believing that God would multiply what I had and it would be enough.

I sent a message to my parents that we still needed more help. Paz didn't yet have her wedding dress, and there were the attendants to consider and the McDougal children who would serve as flower girls and ring bearer. Then, suddenly Robin Layman, Diane's McDougal's sister, had an idea. Her wedding had been postponed at the last minute. Now the dresses intended for her wedding could be loaned to us. The Lord had known our need all along and provided wonderfully just in time.

The church had recently acquired a new organ and, just in time, Mary Hartle, an accomplished American organist, had arrived to play it. We could not have asked for more. God was working it all out.

What excitement there was as the first wedding ever conducted in the Murphy church was about to take place. The space was filled with students, missionaries, relatives, friends, and church members. The reception was held at the Ace Theater building, and immediately afterward, we left for our honeymoon at the Aloha Hotel in downtown Manila.

After the honeymoon, we rejoined the team for a campmeeting in Maria Aurora, Quezon and another campmeeting in Surigao City. After that second campmeeting, we were allowed a brief visit to nearby Gibusong. As you can imagine, I was a happy man. I now had by my side an anointed and wise woman of faith.

13

Into the Fire in Vietnam

Before long, plans were being made for Filipinos to minister in other Asian countries, and Paz and I were praying about what our next step would be. The answer we received surprised us both. God wanted us to go to Vietnam.

It was 1972, we had been married only a matter of weeks, and the war was till raging between South Vietnam (aided by the U.S., the Philippines, and other liberty loving nations) and the Communist North (aided by Russia, China, and other communist countries). Did we want to get in the middle of all that? As we prayed, we received confidence that the God who had joined us as man and wife would never fail us. Although there were many dangers in such an undertaking, God would be with us, providing all our needs and guiding us every step of the way.

When Brother Harold heard from God that we were to go to Vietnam, he couldn't bring himself to tell us. He dreaded taking the responsibility of sending us into the midst of that awful war. More so for newlyweds. He asked the lord to help him.

As he was praying about how to tell us his feelings, Paz and I were praying about how to tell him what we were feeling. This all came to a head one day when he was driving us on a shopping errand. I felt that I had to take this opportunity to express our feelings, and I did. For his part, Brother Harold was very relieved knowing that we had heard from God directly and were in agreement with the assignment.

When the day came for our departure, he drove us to the airport. On the way, he was rather apologetic. He had very little money to give us, and, as always, purposely gave us no contacts. We were fine with that. He was entrusting us into the care of our Protector and Provider, none other than Jehovah-Jireh. We had the assurance that we would be blessed.

Upon landing in Saigon, we went to an inexpensive hotel for the night, and the next day I looked for a directory to find a church we could attend. It would have to be an international church, one where English was spoken. God led us to an international church in Saigon, and it was there that we met missionary Glen Johnson. Glen opened many doors of ministry for us, like a ministry to the Vietnamese soldiers preparing to go into battle, and a ministry that involved getting relief to many needy people. He also introduced us to a very large Alliance church in the city and to many others. This was all very helpful to us and eventually enabled us to carry out a great ministry there in Vietnam.

A continued hotel expense was too much for us, so we were believing God for a miracle. The second Sunday we were in Vietnam, we attended the Alliance services. Seated at the back of the church was a very kind elderly lady who introduced herself to us. As we talked, although we had just met and she really didn't know us, she was led to invite us to come and stay with her during our entire mission in Saigon. As it turned out, she owned a three-story building, and she said she had a room on the third floor reserved just for us. How could we not give thanks to the Lord in such a moment?

The woman gave us her address, and we went there later that day. That evening we slept with the carefree ease of a baby. God had prepared a mission house for us, and our lodging was paid by the Lord Himself. He is indeed awesome!

We ministered in several churches around Saigon and also traveled out to speak to the churches of a tribal group. Once, on a bus back to the city, we were stopped by Vietnamese soldiers. They had encountered a pocket of Vietcong rebels trying to cut the road, and we sat there and prayed as the two groups battled it out. After about an hour of fighting, we were allowed to pass.

14

How Would Marshal Law Affect Us?

On September 21, Ferdinand Marcos, President of the Philippines, declared Martial Law. We were not sure how this would affect us. We had been in Vietnam for three months. Those three months seemed to pass very quickly, and we had many open doors. Then a telegram arrived from the McDougals. It said, "Meet us in the Bangkok airport," and it gave a certain day and a certain time. They were traveling to Jerusalem for a great conference and would be visiting some major cities in Russia along the way, and they were inviting us to accompany them.

We met in Bangkok as planned and all spent the night in a hotel there. The next day, we took a little city tour and then went back to the airport for a flight to New Delhi. Filipinos needed a visa for Russia, and we intended to get one in the Indian capitol.

As it turned out, that next day was a holiday in India, and all embassies were closed. We took the opportunity

How Would Marshal Law Affect Us?

to visit the Taj Mahal. Then, because we now could not meet the group coming from the U.S. and visiting Russia, the decision was made to go directly to Israel and be there ahead of the rest of the group.

Visiting Jerusalem and walking in the places Jesus walked was like a dream. While in Jerusalem, we were able to visit many of the important places to do with Jesus' ministry, places like the Wailing Wall, the Temple Mount, the Mount of Olives, the Garden of Gethsemane, the Garden Tomb, and Mount Zion. We also worshipped with saints from many nations in the famous Saint Peter in Gallicantu Church on Mount Zion. How good God is!

One of the purposes of the great conference in Jerusalem was to begin a ministry there in the Holy City. Many of those who attended stayed on and became part of the wonderful Mount Zion Fellowship, where for many years, people from all over the world found Christ, were filled with the Spirit, and were sent out to the nations. What a privilege it was to be part of that!

15

Walking Where Jesus Walked

When the American team arrived from Russia, we joined them and toured all the important holy places in Jerusalem, Nazareth, and Jericho, and around the Galilee, including Capernaum. We toured such historic places as the Mount of Beatitudes, the Jordan River, and the Sea of Galilee.

After the conference and tour, our plan was to go back to the Philippines. Since Bobby Robinson was with the group, I thought we would be going back with him, but then Brother Harold told us he wanted us to accompany them to the U.S. and said they would apply for visas for us. This was hard for us to believe. We were very excited. Getting a visa to visit the United States was very difficult in those days (as it still is today).

It didn't happen quickly. When the McDougals left for a visit to Scotland on their way to the States, we were left there waiting in Jerusalem. However, it was only a few days before our visas were granted, and we could fly on to the U.S..

16

Arriving in the U.S.

Sister Ruth Heflin, missionary to Jerusalem, suggested that, instead of going into the U.S. through New York, we should enter through Boston since it was less crowded. While we were passing through Immigration and Customs in Boston, we were stopped and Paz was called aside. Something unusual, some leaves, had been discovered in her bag, and officers feared that it might be marijuana. As it turned out, it was only some leaves she had taken from an olive tree in Jerusalem. We were free to go.

We connected to a flight into Washington Dulles Airport, and we wondered how we would get around from there. However, waiting to meet us was Robin Layman, Diane's sister, who had been to the Philippines for a time, so we knew her. What a joy it was to see Robin! She had been so influential in our wedding, preparing the outfits for all the participants, even the little children. We had very little money at the time and were so happy that someone had been sent by God to assist us.

Like a Dream

It was another miracle of God's provision. We would not have been able to afford such beautiful clothes.

We had recently spent several months in war-torn Vietnam, and now, by a miracle, we were going to spend Christmas in America. It seemed like a dream come true.

It was a memorable time indeed. We met so many new people, experienced so many new things (like snow), and received so many wonderful gifts. We were hosted by the Layman family in Hagerstown, Maryland and the McDougal family in Fairmont, West Virginia.

Before long, three more Filipina missionaries who had been sent to South Korea joined us—Sunamita Degorio (Paz's older sister), Emma Querubin, and Aida Padul, and a televised missions conference was held there in Fairmont. We also did meetings in the houses of many hungry people around Fairmont. In later years we were told that these people now made up the backbone of local Spirit-filled churches.

We also had a crusade in nearby Grafton, West Virginia and went to stay with Don and Barbara Ford in their country home. Don had come to the Philippines and helped build the Murphy church and the original concrete block Bible School buildings in Sampaloc. After our meeting, He took us to speak in churches

Arriving in the U.S.

there in Grafton, where we shared about our mission experiences in Vietnam, Indonesia, and Taiwan. It was in Grafton where we met the Charles Dickie family. For several years after that, this family extended financial support to us while we were serving as missionaries in Ecuador. God is so good! He had it all planned out in advance.

17

Visiting the Camp in Ashland, Virginia

On several occasions we were able to visit the camp in Ashland, Virginia, from which many of the missionaries who had served in the Philippines came. These missionaries had been very influential in the great Spiritual Fiesta carried out in our country. Most importantly, there were Pastors Wallace and Edith Heflin and their children, Wallace Jr. and Ruth. The Philippines and we Filipinos had been greatly influenced through their ministries, especially during those great Spiritual Fiesta gatherings. When the elder Wallace Heflin went home to be with the Lord, we didn't hesitate, nor think twice about being at his funeral. However, this time we would have to travel by bus the many hours to Richmond and then on to Ashland, Virginia. The Lord helped us to make the necessary transfer.

Mother Heflin had been taking trips to South America and told her children how hungry the area

Visiting the Camp in Ashland, Virginia

was to hear the Word of God. As a result, Wallace Jr. was led to take a team and do crusades in many South American countries. The response was so great that his team of seven found it difficult to minister to everyone. He called Brother Harold and asked if we could all join them for crusades in the country of Ecuador.

An Unexpected Gift from God

The day Paz and I got married in June of 1972, we already had it in our hearts to go to Vietnam, and our time there was a great blessing. But Vietnam also blessed us in another way, a very unexpected way.

Sister Diane had warned us that because we were on a mission, we would have to be careful to avoid a pregnancy, but as careful as we tried to be, by August Paz sensed that she was, as we say here in the Philippines, "in a family way." At first, we kept this joyous news to ourselves as long as possible, but along the way—from Vietnam, to Thailand, to India, to Israel and on to the U.S.—it became apparent to all that we were expecting our first child.

We were not alarmed by this turn of events. We had been taught to live by faith. If God loved us and made miraculous provision for our every need, He would do the same for our child. This child would be blessed, just as we were blessed. We were in God's hands.

Now, as plans were being made for the team to go to Ecuador, it was decided that Paz should stay behind in

Fairmont with the McDougal family. The rigors of the trip might be too much for an expectant mother. The rest of us would join the mission to Ecuador, and our eight added to the Heflin seven would be more effective.

Leaving Paz behind was not a good feeling. We had become a team. But going to South America seemed like a rare opportunity, and we were all excited. At the same time, it was wonderful for me to know that Paz would be well cared for before, during, and after the delivery. God is good! Our mission to South America was about to begin.

19

The Amazing Miracles of Ecuador

Our first stop was in Quito, the capital of Ecuador, a quaint city situated high in the Andes Mountains. God was performing many miracles in the crusades, so many sick attended. One of them was the wife of a wealthy car dealer. They were Europeans, originally from Checkoslovakia, but had immigrated to Ecuador after the Second World War. Their names were Otto and Lily Kladenski. Sister Lily was suffering from severe rheumatoid arthritis, which doctors attributed to the fact that, as a young Jewish lady, she had been interred in Hitler's death camps.

The Kladenskis were an amazing family. They had taken his earnings from car sales and her inheritance from her father and built a beautiful campground eighteen kilometers outside of Quito in the little village of La Merced. They called it Campamento Nueva Vida (New Life Camp). They asked if our

The Amazing Miracles of Ecuador

team could come out there one day and pray for them. We were only too happy to comply.

The five-hectare grounds of New Life Camp had been beautifully landscaped, many buildings had been erected, and others were in progress. Among the buildings were a dining hall with seating for two hundred and fifty people, a guest house with four lovely rooms (each with a private bathroom), many dormitories, a large games room for indoor activities, classrooms, a kiosk for a little camp store, a chapel, a director's house with several bedrooms, and a house with rooms for the ground's keepers.

There were volleyball and basketball courts, soccer fields, a bonfire area, two fish ponds, and a swimming pool. All of this had been built with their hard-earned money, and yet the family was now unsure about what exactly to do with these beautiful facilities. A program of sorts had been started by an American group, but when no one was happy with the results, the program was abandoned.

We all testified to them about what was happening in the Ashland camp and what had been happening in the camp meetings in the Philippines. These had first been conducted in Sampaloc, Tanay, Rizal, but after the Spiritual Fiesta they had expanded to

Like a Dream

Quezon City, Surigao City, and Quezon Province. CTTP had been granted the use of public facilities in both Quezon City and Surigao City for these summer meetings.

After sharing with the Kladenski family our experiences and our vision for their camp, we split up and went to all parts of New Life Camp to pray, and as we prayed, we each began to feel the same thing. The Lord was arranging for the members of our team to take control of that amazing property and use it for His glory. It all happened so quickly and so easily the we were taken by surprise.

The McDougals could not stay just then, so Jay Rawlings (a member of the Heflin group, who had been sent ahead to set up the meetings in Ecuador and who already knew the most important pastors) agreed to stay and take charge temporarily. His wife Meridel and two young sons who were in the camp in Ashland would soon join him. They asked me, Sunamita, Aida, and Emma to stay too, and Diane's two sisters, Robin and Cheri, also stayed. Our job would be to visit all the churches, announcing the upcoming camp program, and then to serve as the first camp counselors.

So, instead of returning to the Philippines or staying in the U.S., we stayed on in Ecuador. Beulah

Louise, our beautiful daughter, was born on April 5, and by May, Paz and the baby were ready to join us in the work of Ecuador. An exciting new chapter in our lives had begun, a chapter that would be both memorable and productive.

20

New Life Camp Activities

Our duties at New Life Camp were many and varied. We were the camp counselors and teachers when camp was in session. What did it mean to be a camp counselor? Each counselor was in charge of one room full of campers. In the case of the ladies, this was a room with eight beds. For the men, it was twelve. We slept in the same room with our campers, escorted them to their various activities, worked with them when it was their turn to clean the dining hall and wash the dishes, oversaw their comportment, and even their sports activities, and dealt with any necessary disciplinary issues. In short, we were their parents while they were in the camp.

I was often chosen to oversee the male counselors and was later chosen at times to take charge of the entire program when Brother Harold and other missionaries were away.

What did it mean to be a teacher at New Life Camp? There were many classes and services, and we could be called upon at any given time to give a teaching or to preach in one of the services. The Ecuadorian young people were so eager to learn that this was always a treat.

When camp was not in session (during scheduled school days), we prepared food for and served Christian groups who rented the camp. We even did the maintenance work and prepared and served meals to save costs. But we also used the camp as a center from which to do missionary work all over Ecuador and the rest of South America. We also served as teachers for the missionary training center attended by Ecuadorians, Colombians, and Venezuelans, even some from the U.S.

One year, when camp was not in session, we all split up into four teams and conducted crusades around Ecuador. I was the leader of one of those teams. My team, which included five camp ministers, also included Sister Aida. She not only sang; she also played the guitar very well, so that was a great blessing to the team.

I requested the use of the tent the camp had purchased for outdoor activities and in which the nightly meetings were held during camptime. That tent was set up in Tulcan, Puyo, Riobamba, and the border town of Ipiales, Colombia. We also had a crusade in the coastal town of Manta in an open-air plaza. The tent was a drawing card,

Like a Dream

and in Tulcan, our first meeting place, it was packed. There were many miracles of healing, and many people came to Christ, accepting Him as personal Lord and Savior.

Back at home in the camp, all the staff members had regular days of fasting and daily hours of prayer, but now we went to our assigned areas weeks before the crusade and began the preparations, working with local churches. Those crusades left a mark on many Ecuadorian towns.

At one point, early on, back in the capital, we met Pastor Zenon Rivera from the Vicentina, a southern part of the city, and he invited us to his church. We gave our testimonies and shared some of the things God had been doing for us and prayed for him and his people to receive the Holy Spirit. Only later I came to know that it was their introduction into the things of the Spirit. Cordero De Dios (Lamb of God), as the church is known, now has thirty congregations, ten of them in the capital city, and their main church, which they call *el coliseum* (the coliseum), now seats more than two thousand people.

As a side note, most of the Ecuadorian people had never seen an Asian and insisted on calling us *los Chinos* (those Chinese). They meant nothing bad by this, and we were wonderfully received everywhere we went.

New Life Camp Activities

At one point a young American named Kepler Nigh joined us in Ecuador. A skilled photographer, he was also from Fairmont, and we had met his mother. She had become a very good friend to Paz and was very helpful after the baby was born. God has His wonderful people everywhere.

21

Reaching Out to Other Nations

When we first arrived in Ecuador, none of us spoke Spanish, so we had to use interpreters. However, we Filipinos had the advantage of the many Spanish words in our Filipino dialects. The spelling was different, but the many years of Spanish rule over the Philippines had given us a definite head start. The Lord helped us, and we were soon preaching and teaching in Spanish. Fortunately I had also studied a little Spanish in both high school and college.

In time, Paz led a team to Colombia, while others went to Peru, and Venezuela. At one point Brother Harold and I took a quick trip to many of the South American countries. Since I knew more Spanish, I served as his interpreter. We preached in Peru, Bolivia, Chile, Argentina, Uruguay, and Brazil before returning to the camp in Ecuador.

Within Ecuador itself, one of our main areas of focus was to help Ecuadorian Christians be filled with the Spirit and go back to stir up their churches.

Reaching Out to Other Nations

Since we met many of the pastors and their people in the camp, they knew us, and we were welcomed all over the country and hosted in their homes. It was a wonderful time of ministry within and without that quaint Andean nation.

It was during our time at Campamento Nueva Vida that I had one of my most memorable experiences. Brother Harold had asked me to minister in one of the evening services. There were several hundred young people in attendance, and a tent had been erected beside one of the camp lakes to accommodate them all. A mighty move of God came that night, and we had an unusual outpouring. Dozens came to the altar to be saved, and many more were filled with the Holy Spirit and spoke in tongues under the power of God.

On two consecutive evenings we had a similar outpouring of the Holy Spirit. There was so much hunger and thirst among those campers, and they lingered long in prayer, seeking God's presence and soaking it in. In Joel 2:28-30, the Lord said:

And afterward,
 I will pour out my Spirit on all people.
Your sons and daughters will prophesy,

Like a Dream

> *your old men will dream dreams,*
> *your young men will see visions.*
> *Even on my servants, both men and women,*
> *I will pour out my Spirit in those days.*
> *I will show wonders in the heavens*
> *and on the earth.*

He was fulfilling His Word before our very eyes.

22

Back in the Philippines

In April of 1977, Paz and I felt it was time to return to the Philippines. We had been in Ecuador for four years. Beulah was already four years old and spoke fluent Spanish. (Later she would marry and move to Florida, where she encountered many Latinos, so her Spanish came in handy.)

We arrived back in the Philippines in time for the Christ to the Philippines Annual Convention. It was great to be back. It was just the four of us now, the three Colosagas and Aida. Emma had married Bruce Behnken from Dayton, Ohio, and Sunamita had married Juan Cuello from Guayaquil, Ecuador, and they now had their own ministries. We spent a lot of time sharing what God had done on our various mission trips, to Indonesia, Taiwan, South Vietnam, South Korea, Ecuador, and the other South American countries. It was an exciting time.

I had a strange experience when I went back to visit my mother. She spoke no Tagalog and no English, only

Like a Dream

Ilocano. It had been so long since I spoke my native Ilocano that I had a hard time communicating with her. Still, it was good to be back with people we loved and who loved us, and it was good to be back in Lal-lo again.

I was led to express great gratitude to my father, Emilio, who had been a spiritual pillar for the Colosaga family during the four years we had been in Ecuador. He had been very faithful to write us letters, always filled with words of encouragement and insights into God's Word, reflecting his long-standing role as Sunday school teacher. Those letters would sometimes take up to a month to reach us. Because of the very poor phone service in the camp in La Merced, only once we were able to connect by telephone from the Mission House in Ecuador to the Mission House in Quezon City, and I had a chance to greet my sister, who was working with Christ to the Philippines at the time.

After Lal-lo, it was time for us to visit the island of Gibusong, home of Paz, and we stayed there for nearly a month. My younger brother and my sister Visie accompanied us. The Colosagas and the Degorios and related families had never stopped praying for us during the years we had been abroad and had a great part in the harvests of souls reaped.

23

Getting Back to Work

After visiting our families, we traveled back to Manila. It was time to get back to work.

We settled in with the Robinsons and the other Filipino workers (Brother Bobby was, by then, our missionary director). At first, we just did odd jobs, whatever we were needed for. Eventually we both got involved in teaching at the Asian Hope Bible School, which had been rebuilt in Tanay, and Paz did a lot of cooking. She had learned from Sister Diane at the camp in Ecuador, where they had to prepare for hundreds of youth, and from Mom McDougal in Fairmont. All things work together for good!

In 1978, I was elected to the National Board of CTTP and was appointed Assistant Director. For two years I pastored the CTTP church in Kamuning and, at the same time, served in the national office. It was good preparation for what the Lord had planned for us. Surprisingly, by 1981, during our yearly convention, I was elected as the National Director of Christ of the Philippines and served in that post for the next thirty years.

Like a Dream

In 2000, after much prayer, I decided it was time to let others take over. For the next six years, I let my good friend, Danny de Guzman, cover that role. Danny had been my classmate in Bible school, and we both graduated in the first batch of students from Tanay, Rizal in 1968.

The two of us were assigned, I to Malolos and he to Calumpit. It was a very difficult assignment for me. The people of Malolos spoke a very pure Tagalog, and I was certainly not a pure Tagalog speaker. I struggled to form complete sentences in the language, let alone preach in Tagalog. Consequently, I didn't stay very long in that assignment. Aside from the language problem, it seemed to me that we did not have nearly enough training in pastoral work.

I also tried to serve in Santa Maria, Laguna. My failures drew me closer to the Lord and I sought Him more. As always, He was there to guide us, help us, and keep us moving forward, never giving up. Eventually, I was over all the churches of CTTP, not just one. What a miracle!

24

The Miracles of Those Years

Those years of service were memorable, and many great things happened. At first, I wondered how we could possibly do such a big job. We had so little income, so few pastors, and so little experience. But then I felt God telling me to trust Him, and when I did, He began to work wonders.

For instance, one day I received a phone call from an American evangelist from Seattle, Richard McNeely. I didn't know this man. He said he had come to the Philippines at the invitation of a pastor in Samar. Strangely, even though they had agreed on a date and time of arrival, the pastor from Samar had failed to show up at the airport to receive the evangelist and his wife, Donna. They had checked into a local hotel the day before and there, in a directory, he had found a listing for Christ to the Philippines. Fortunately, I just happened to be in the office when he called, and so I learned about their predicament.

Like a Dream

As I prayed, I felt that this was no mistake. I offered to pick them up at their hotel, and we went to have lunch together. Even though I didn't know these people, the Holy Spirit was drawing me to them.

Fortunately, I had learned to drive, and after lunch I took them by to see our Mission House in Quezon City. While there in the office, we arranged meetings for them in the Murphy, Signal Village, and Bangkal churches. These were the only three churches we had at the time in the Metro Manila area.

As we talked, the evangelist shared with me his vision of doing evangelistic work in the Philippines, particularly in Metro Manila. His goal was to establish ten churches. He wanted more than to just conduct crusades. He wanted to see churches established in the targeted areas. I sensed that we needed to grab hold of this opportunity and work with these people. They were new to our city, but they had a great vision.

After the church meetings had ended, we made plans for the evangelist to come back and do exactly what God had put in his heart to do. It was now my responsibility to pray and find the will of God for what cities would be targeted.

This American evangelist would be coming back again and again and bringing a team with him, and there was more. Aside from raising the necessary funds for the crusades, he also assumed the responsible for a designated monthly allowance for pastors and their families to follow up the results of the meetings and also for the rental for a house for the pastor. This house would double as a meeting place for the new church.

Not only were these arrangements planned; they were also executed, and the result was nine churches added. These were in Cainta, Taytay, Binangonan, Malabon, Mandaluyong, Taguig, Pasay, Valley View, and Nagcarlan, Laguna.

Other churches were planted by the pastors who were caring for these nine churches. These were in Pangasinan, particularly Cabangan, San Pedro, Burgos in Umingan town, and Lupao in Nueva Ecijah. It was my obligation to look for men and women who would be able to pastor these new congregations, and thank God, at His direction, I was able to find a pastor for each and every church. These churches were all growing, and some of them were even able to have their own church building and other facilities.

Crusades were also held in Catarman, Northern Samar, and Panobo, Davao Del Norte, all with CTTP pastors. How wonderful is our God!

25

The Seeds of Worship and Praise Missionary Training Center

About 1988, I received a letter from Taiwan from a brother named Pastor Abel Yeh. I knew nothing about Pastor Yeh. He had gotten my name from Pastor Peter, a missionary from Hong Kong who was working in Taipei. Pastor Peter had visited us, and, as usual, I took him around to speak at several of our churches in Metro Manila. I asked him to speak in a new church in Malabon. He not only spoke; he officiated the baptism of new believers.

The letter from Pastor Abel was written by Deborah, his niece. She was an English teacher, and she was helping him because his English was not very good. She said that Pastor Abel wanted to come to the Philippines with a team of five. We gladly received them.

Before coming, Pastor Abel had a vision of a man with a mustache in a green pickup truck meeting them

The Seeds of Worship and Praise Missionary Training Center

at the airport, and when I met them at the airport in a green Ford truck, it was a confirmation to all of them that God was in their plan.

After that, Pastor Abel visited us a number of times. Following my usual routine, I would take him around to our various churches. During one of these visits, he spoke to me about something the Lord had laid on his heart. He had a burden to put up a missionary training center. At first, I struggled with this idea because Christ to the Philippines already had its Bible school in Tanay, Rizal, and pastors were being equipped there for the organization. Both Paz and I were teaching there. But as we waited upon the Lord, He showed us that He was opening this door and would indeed make this vision come to pass.

Pastor Abel and his people had been praying about buying a property somewhere in Metro Manila where this training center could operate. We began to look around and found several lots in Quezon City where such a facility could be built. We also looked for available properties in the areas where other churches were being planted.

One day I spoke about this search to the Nepomuceno family, a pioneer family from Pasay. On one occasion, when I spoke at the church they were attending, Sister

Like a Dream

Lina invited me to have lunch afterward with the family. When I later heard that this family had moved to Parañaque, we felt led to visit them. They were now living in a subdivision called Countryside Village, Sunvalley, Parañaque City. While we visited, we asked them if there were any available properties nearby.

As we looked together around that village and adjacent villages, we were directed to a property for sale at 309 Hummingbird Street. We located the owner of the property and discovered that he was moving to the U.S. We negotiated with the caretaker to buy the 240-square-meter property. The sale price was 800,000 Pesos, plus 20,000 for the telephone line that was already installed.

I sensed the Lord telling me that this location would not only be a training center, but also a church. Christ to the Philippines did not yet have a ministry in Parañaque. Eventually, the deal was done, and, with the agreement of Pastor Abel, the property was deeded to Christ to the Philippines.

With the church planting in my heart, even before moving into the unfinished building, I decided to start a Bible study. We started with Sister Lina and her family and the members of my family I had asked to come from the province and serve as carpenters and workers on the construction of the building.

The Seeds of Worship and Praise Missionary Training Center

As another confirmation that we were on the right property, the Lord gave the brothers from Taiwan a vision of two fruit trees. One was seasonal, and the other had fruit all year round. Sure enough, we had two such trees on the property. The seasonal one was a chico tree, and the one bearing all year round was a kamias. Until now, we still have the kamias and have gotten fruit from it often through the years. There was so much fruit that we shared it with the church members.

26

The Battle for the Vision

An interesting incident happened during the construction of the building in Parañaque. When the Catholic homeowners heard that we were building a mission house and a church there, they got together and protested to the president of the subdivision. He, in turn, insisted on having a meeting with me and Pastor Abel and the other officers of Countryside Village, and the meeting was held in his house.

The president began the meeting by insisting that the construction be halted. Pastor Abel answered him, "God told us to buy the property and to build on it a missionary training center. We cannot stop."

Hearing the results of the meeting, the homeowners circulated a petition, got it signed by the majority of the families, and sent it off to the city engineer, objecting to the construction and asking that it be stopped immediately. Thankfully, construction had already begun. We had legally purchased the property, and we had a permit from the city engineer for the building. We were confident that God would intervene. I circulated this news to all of the pastors of Christ to the Philippines and urged them to fervently pray for God to give us favor. They did, and God did His part. The construction went on unhindered.

Two other visions the Taiwanese brothers received had confirmed the property. In one vision, the property was seen between two streams. I had to look at Google Maps to be sure this vision was true. Until today, those two streams exist, and during heavy downpours, they clog up, and a bridge at the lower end of the subdivision floods.

In another vision, a sign with the sun and rays emanating out from it were seen. This is a sign for Barangay Sun Valley that is very prominent at the entrance of our village. Very soon we were training Christian workers in a two-year course, and since 1994, when we graduated our first batch of trainees, there have now been 185 pastors, teachers, evangelists, and church workers who have passed through this biblical missionary course.

The training center operates on a free board and lodging basis. The students pay nothing while attending the Bible training. We urge them that by the time they finish their studies, they should believe God to meet all their needs in the ministry. We have many testimo-

Like a Dream

nies to the goodness of the Lord in this regard, and we always look forward to hearing these testimonies. The graduates also send back reports of souls being saved, bodies being healed, and believers receiving the power of the Holy Spirit.

As I write this, we are now on our 15th batch in the training center. We have only nine students enrolled this time, but we are believing that they will be instrumental in the Body of Christ in the days ahead. God is so good!

27

Fruit That Remains

As I was writing this in August of 2024, Jay dee Kilayon from Kalinga texted that he was going to Bohol to assist the ministry there. Jay is from the 14th batch. He was not sure whether he would pursue ministry after graduation, but God showed him, through circumstances, what His will was. He had taken an exam, hoping to continue another pursuit, but the fact that he was unable to pass the exam was a sign to him from God that he was to serve Him.

This was an answer to prayer because Tom and Myra Ridenour, Christ to the Philippines missionaries to Bohol, had been requesting workers from the Bible school. I told them we would pray about it because only a few students from Christ to the Philippines itself have come to the training center. Generally speaking, only a third or less of those who have enrolled are from our own organization. And, unless a graduate makes the decision to work with the organization, it is not our policy to assign them

Like a Dream

to a Christ to the Philippines church. We rejoiced in the decision of Jay dee Kilayon to aid the great work in Bohol.

The amazing thing about the work in Parañaque is that from the beginning, the Taiwanese believers from Pastor Abel Yeh's church funded the work. From time to time, some donations came in from other interested groups, but the Taiwanese brothers carried the bulk of the financial burden.

They bought the lot, funded the construction of the building, and financed the monthly budget of the school. This was what allowed us to offer free board and lodging for students and to provide a teacher's allowance.

Before graduation, each batch has been required to do a two-month-long exposure trip, even if it consisting of practical ministry in their home churches, and part of this program was also funded by the Taiwanese believers. What a miracle! To God be all the glory!

28

Meeting the Ridenours

In 2012, the Lord allowed me to visit the U.S. with two other pastors from Christ ton the Philippines, and I took the opportunity to go to Maryland to visit our friends and supporters and the Philippine Missions base in Hagerstown.

Tom Ridenour was the one who picked me up at Washington's Dulles International Airport. We had been corresponding through social media, but I had not yet met him personally. I knew his parents who had come to the Philippines in 1972, just about the time Paz and I were leaving for Vietnam. Although Tom and his twin brother, Tim, were born while their parents were serving as missionaries to the Philippines, Paz and I had been away in Ecuador at the time.

Meeting Tom and Tim was providential. Tom welcomed me into their home and drove me to my appointments. In the process, we were able to share a lot about what God had done and was still doing in the Philippines. The result was that Tom and his wife

Like a Dream

Myra felt a calling to full-time ministry and, better yet, to ministry in the Philippines.

The Ridenours are now in their tenth year as missionaries to the Philippines, and God has helped them to plant three churches on the island of Bohol. That province had been known as one of the hardest in the nation to reach for the Gospel of Christ, but God has given them favor.

Each of their three churches has corresponding outreaches, and we have tried to do our part by sending graduates who are willing to help them. As I mentioned before, this has sometimes been a struggle for us, as not many youth were coming to the training center from the Christ to the Philippines churches. When young people come to us for training from other churches, we don't feel that we have the freedom to assign them work after graduation. It has, therefore, been our policy to let them go back their own churches or organizations. If a graduate from another church really wants to work with us, they must seek permission from their home church. With the 2024 batch, for the first time, Tom and Myra were able to send three of their own young people for training.

The work in Bohol has become a pacesetter. In a few years' time, they not only have been able to plant churches; they have also been able to provide good buildings for their churches, as well as housing for their pastors. Tom has been blessed with three houses. One of them was called the Chocolate House, after the famous Chocolate Hills of Bohol.

When Tom and Myra first arrived, it was our privilege to host them, and it has been a privilege to continue extending help to them in terms of advice and recommending pastors who could visit them. Presently we have three graduates who are helping them, and in the past, we helped them with two workers while they were in their pioneering stages. In all, seven workers have been assigned to help the work in Bohol, and the work in Bohol continues to prosper despite the many challenges they face.

29

The Walking Bible

I must mention one American evangelist who visited us often through the years. Fred Jensen has long been known as The Walking Bible. He got this title because, as he preached, his words, from start to finish, were taken directly from Bible verses. Fred and his wife Darlene began visiting the Philippines way back before Paz and I left for the mission in Vietnam, and they continued to come for many years, taking an active part in evangelistic crusades and in the ministry to churches. They inspired the members of our churches to recognize the need to win souls and deliver people from sicknesses. I was blessed to accompany them in several of these meetings. Some were in cities and some in remote areas. They, as Americans, visited many more parts of the Philippines than I, a Filipino, and all to fulfill the Great Commission.

Fred and Darlene also assisted other organizations outside of Christ to the Philippines and, in doing so, traveled to many parts of Luzon and also to the Visayas and Mindanao. Beginning in the early 1970s, they came two or three times a year, even living for a while in the Philippines in Quezon City. Such was their love for the country.

In the beginning, Brother Fred would play something on his trumpet before he preached, and Sister Darlene would follow with a song. "I had nothing but heartache and troubles, but now I have everything." Dozens of Christ to the Philippines churches were blessed by their ministry.

The Jensens were also very generous with their financial support. They donated to many church building projects. Closer to home, they donated to the tiling of the ground floor of the Worship and Praise Missionary Training Center here in Parañaque. These are just a few ways in which they helped the Christ to the Philippines ministry and others, all for the glory of God.

With Fred now in his nineties, the Jensens travel less these days, but they left an indelible mark upon the Philippines and upon our hearts.

30

The Korean Connection

A Korean missionary couple living in the Philippines, Rev. Hoon Cha and Smn. Anna, became our first link to IGM (International Grace Ministries) led by Rev. James Shin. Rev. Shin and his church are a branch of Grace Ministry International of Fulton, California. Their congregation, made up mostly of Korean Americans, was using the discipleship method known as D12.[1] They introduced us to this method, and it was so well received that it was adopted in most of our CTTP churches.

The D12 method involves the Encounter Program carried out in local churches and Freedom seminars. Using this method caused a remarkable growth in our churches, both spiritually in numbers. We formed a group of ten churches from within and without CTTP. They were CTTP Rock, CTTP SVC, CTTP Nagcarlan,

---

1. The D12 method of discipleship is a system where a leader or pastor disciples a small group of 12 people who, in turn, are equipped and sent out to disciple 12 others. Based on the biblical model of Jesus and his twelve apostles, the method emphasizes relational training and multiplication to expand the church. It is also referred to as the Government of 12 (G12).

The Korean Connection

CTTP Batasan, CTTP Parañaque, Iriga Praise Church, IGM Davao, IGM Cotabato, and IGM Manila. Twice yearly, an event named Tres Diaz is held, in St. Michael, Antipolo and also in Davao City.

Tres Diaz is the name being used in the U.S., but Pastor Shin decided to call the event here in the Philippines the Philippines Glow of Love (PGL). This program has helped our churches grow, with its emphasis on closer bonding among the members.

It was because of this Korean connection that Paz and I were able to make two trips to the U.S., joining tour groups from Thailand, Myanmar, Scotland, Korea and China.

PGL is now being held here in the Philippines during All Souls Day and Holy Week because these are vacation days and so are suitable for the three days of the event. We have also now held two Sequelas, ten year anniversary celebrations.

31

Dealing with the Unlucky Number 13

When it came time to accepting applications for the 13th batch of students, we experienced a time of confusion in which we were not sure of the immediate continuation of the program. This confusion had to do with the number 13. I was not a superstitious person, but I suddenly remembered stories about Friday the 13th and the fact that the Philippines, like many other countries, avoids having a thirteenth floor in high-rise buildings. Thirteen is clearly not a lucky number.

The idea came to me to cancel the 13th batch and move on to the 14th. In the end, the Lord led me to move ahead with the 13th batch, believing that He could make everything right, despite the superstitions of men.

We began accepting students, and the Lord sent us a good group of twelve or thirteen. Even one young lady came from Vietnam. It was the first

Dealing with the Unlucky Number 13

time we had ever admitted students from a foreign country.

This happened because someone we didn't even know, a pastor whose wife was an Overseas Filipino Workers or OFW came in contact with Pastor Tony of the Rhema Church in Vietnam. Pastor Tony had a prospective student whose name was Sarah, and Sarah was desirous of being trained at a missionary school. She arrived with Pastor Tony to Manila one day before we started classes, and we picked them up at the airport.

Pastor Tony spoke English, but Sarah knew only a little. Still, she was very determined to fulfill God's calling in her life. Amazingly, she finished the course, but, of course, she experienced many hardships along the way. She had to make a double effort to learn English at the same time, and, being a foreigner, her visa was not an easy issue either.

In that 13th batch, we also admitted some older students, more or less in their forties. This was good because they served as Mom and Dad to the younger students.

During the 13th batch training period, we celebrated Christmas together for the first time with our students by taking them all out to a buffet lunch. It was, for them, a moment of great excitement, and God provided

Like a Dream

for the bill. Usually, we had prepared a Christmas dinner at home, with Paz's cooking being greatly appreciated. But going out didn't cost that much more, and they all enjoyed having an "all-you-can-eat" meal. Many of them had never experienced such a treat and didn't know how much to get on their plates. We advised them not to take too much of any one thing and quickly fill up, to just try a little at first to see what they liked and then get more. Everyone enjoyed the experience.

During the summer break that year we sent the students out on missions to the places they believed God was leading them. Sarah wanted to spend her summer in Vietnam. Because she was a good friend of Jonalyn Castro from Mindoro Oriental, the two of them teamed up for the summer mission. Because it was a school project, they only had to pay one-way for the trip. What a wonderful time it was when they all returned with good reports of what God had done!

32

Beulah Louise

I have already related how Paz got pregnant in Vietnam and carried the baby through many nations and then how the decision was made for her to stay behind in the U.S. to give birth while the rest of us traveled to Ecuador. When that baby was born on April 5 of 1973 in Fairmont, West Virginia, we named her Beulah Louise.

The name Beulah had a specific meaning to the children of Israel, but we just thought it was a beautiful name for a beautiful baby. Her middle named was Louise after our U.S. hostess, Helen Louise McDougal, who took such good care of them both during those months we were separated. Beulah was indeed a gift from God.

During the years we spent in Ecuador, Beulah became fluent in Spanish. Then, after we returned to the Philippines, she became fluent in Tagalog. And, of course, she was fluent in English. She did well through kindergarten and grade school and was then enrolled

Like a Dream

in Roosevelt College as it was closest to where we were living at the time.

When I accepted the pastorship of the Kamuning Church, Beulah had to transfer for a time to a closer school. Then she did her first two years of college at Trinity College in Quezon City.

About that time, it was suggested that, because she was a U.S. citizen, having been born there, she could transfer to college in the U.S. We had a friend in Jacksonville, Florida, Leny Labad, so Beulah finished her nursing course there in Jacksonville. After graduating, she began her career, married, and has prospered. God is so good. He loves each one of us. WE thank God for Beulah.

33

The Miracle of Hannah

God sees every longing of our hearts. Despite the fact that we had one daughter and were taking care of dozens of students at any given time and treating them like our own children, Paz and I had a longing for another child of our own.

Beulah was now so far away that we didn't get to visit her much. She and her husband were doing well, she was making strides in her chosen profession as a nurse, and we were grateful to the Lord for His blessings on their lives, but we somehow still longed for another child. God answered that prayer with a miracle named Hannah Luzviminda Bundoc.[1]

Hannah's mother was a single lady with a position of responsibility who found herself in the unenviable position of expecting a child. She felt that she could not offer her unborn child the future he or she deserved, so she confided in church leaders and asked for prayer. The

---

1. In time, we made a special trip to a court in Cabanatuan, and through a process, her family name was changed to Colosaga.

person she confided in happened to be a good friend of ours, and she knew of our longing for another child of our own. She asked us if Paz would maybe like to care for this child. We were overjoyed. This was the answer to our prayers.

Our commitment was to care for Hannah until she finished high school, but gradually she became a real part of the family. She grew into a lovely teenager and then into a lovely lady, finishing her high school with flying colors and graduating from the university Cum Laude.

A week before Hannah graduated from her Human Resources course, she was admitted as an employee of Citibank, where she is currently employed, and until now, she is with us, helping me to write this book and blessing us in so many other ways. We have two beautiful daughters, Beulah Louise and Hannah Luzviminda, and we love them both, along with all of the spiritual sons and daughters we have been blessed to nurture through the years.

It must be noted that Hannah's biological mother has been a part of her life from the beginning, has been a member in good standing in our congregation for many years, and continues to do well in the Lord.

34

Our Trip to Vietnam, Cambodia, and Thailand

Paz, Hannah, and I were praying to be able to go for a mission trip to Vietnam, Cambodia, and Thailand. Paz and I had not been back to Vietnam since the four months we spent there as a young married couple during the War. In Cambodia, there were two of our lady missionaries already working at the Functional English Center, and we wanted to join them.

When Sister Diane McDougal heard about the plan, she said she would like to go with us and also invited Sister Peggy (Boutchyard) Kulynych to go along. It was really a wonderful trip. We were privileged to be traveling with two of those who had founded Christ to the Philippines.

After we completed our trip in those three countries, Diane and Peggy planned to go on to Australia for a short trip before the 50th Annual Convention of Christ in the Philippines, which was a big celebration for the organization.

Like a Dream

In Vietnam, Cambodia, and Thailand, the Lord allowed us to visit churches. In Vietnam, we spoke at a church in Long Ann, a church that was meeting at Sarah's house, a church in Ho Chi Minh City, the Rhema Church of Pastor Tony, and one of his other outreaches. What a privilege to be able to preach in such a restricted country! God allowed us to be a witness that even if His people go through some sort of persecution, His Church prevails.

In Cambodia, we met the children coming to the English Functional Center and were able to minister to them. Our two lady missionaries were serving as teachers there under Ethnos Asia, another missionary agency founded by and headed by a Filipino.

Evelyn was from the 9th batch, and Chebot was from the 12th batch. Evelyn had visited Thailand with Christine, but after two months, Christine had decided to come home, thinking that was not the ministry God had called her to. That left Evelyn without a partner. As she was praying about where she was to go, the director of Ethnos Asia made her an offer. There was a need for out-of-school children in Siem Reap, Cambodia to learn English, and they were looking for someone to start the school. Evelyn responded to this opportunity, and had now been in Cambodia for seven years, doing a wonderful work, a work she loves. God has brought to her hundreds of children, and she has had the opportunity to teach them Bible stories and also to witness to their parents and point them toward salvation and deliverance.

Evelyn came back to visit Worship and Praise Missionary Training Center, and we gave her the opportunity to speak to the students about the ministry in Cambodia. Chebot was one of the students and was so touched by Evelyn's words that she approached Paz later, saying that she felt a strong call to become a missionary to Cambodia.

Another graduate, Danmel, also indicated his desire for missions and asked if it was possible for him to join FEC (Functional English Center). He was a talented painter and painted the frame we have in the background of our meeting hall here in the training center. According to him, when he was planning to come to the Bible school, his father was not happy about it. He said, "We did not do all this to get you a good education in architecture, just so you could waste your time going to some "mission." But Danmel felt a very strong pull from God to serve Him. Even before Danmel came to the Bible school, he had the experience of going to the Muslim provinces here in the Philippines and

Like a Dream

preaching the Gospel. The director of Ethnos Asia approved of him joining the effort in Siem Reap, but first wanted him to get some more exposure in Thailand. We continue to pray that those who come to our training program will hear the call of God to missions, and that His call will become a reality in their lives. We regularly increase our units on the subject of missions. It is what we have experienced and has always been the reason for the Missionary Training Center concept.

Sarah has notified us that there is another prospective student from Vietnam, another young lady. The situation is similar. This student also doesn't speak English well. My assignment to Sarah was to teach the girl English before she gets to the Philippines. She is planning to come in the 16th batch.

35

Sister Peggy's Contribution

The mention of Sister Peggy Kulynych in that last chapter leads me to say something more of her contribution to the ministry here in the Philippines. As a young single person, she had served for a time with the McDougals as an evangelist. Then she married Abe Kulynych (who often helped secure equipment for the Philippine work and also visited in the early years. That's how he and Peggy met.)

After raising her two boys and the passing of Abe, Peggy decided to visit us again during that 50th Anniversary celebration. Others who attended were Ben Yu, Sonny Largado, Bobby and Rita Robinson, Abie Kulynych (Peggy's eldest son, who is a pastor in New Jersey), Dan McDougal (eldest son of the McDougals), Pam (Edgell) Marocco (who had also served CTTP in her youth, and her son, Mark.

Sister Peggy enjoyed her visit so much that she went home, sold her house, and came back to the Philippines to live. Her plan was to do evangelism, teach, and serve

Like a Dream

in any way she could. She rented a house in Marikina and fixed it up to her liking. I and some of our students helped out.

Sister Peggy was one of the speakers at our Ilocano District Convention in Conner, Apayao. That Sunday I assigned the various speakers to preach in our churches in the area: Paddaoan, Catub, Lenneng, Taracay, Badduat, and Malaweg. Peggy preached in the largest of the churches, Palan-ag.

After coming back to Manila, Peggy went to Bohol to preach there with the Ridenours. Then, without warning, Covid struck, and Peggy was advised by her embassy to go back to the U.S. Because she was otherwise quarantined at her Marikina home, she reluctantly agreed. Her thought was to return just as soon as possible, but after the Covid crisis was over, her health suddenly began to deteriorate. Other than speak to our convention online, she has not been able to return.

I must divulge that Sister Peggy was instrumental in acquiring a vehicle for the ministry of Worship and Praise Missionary Training Center, and we are grateful for all of her various contributions.

36

Fruit in Vietnam

Sarah, from the 13th batch, is very involved in the ministry in Vietnam. She went back to Vietnam after the pandemic. She had made the 13th batch special because it was the first time a student had come from abroad to study and be equipped.

When the two-year course was over, and she was about to graduate, COVID-19 struck here in Metro Manila, there was a lockdown, and travel restrictions were imposed. Using face masks and getting the vaccination were requirements. We, too, were locked down in our home and could not hold any face-to-face services. All our services had to be online. Many government restrictions were put in place in an attempt to gain control of the spread of the virus.

Graduation had been rescheduled for May that year, but as we were preparing for that event, the pandemic struck again, and all the students had to return to their homes, for we were forbidden to hold classes.

Like a Dream

One student, Jonalyn, nearly missed the last trip to Mindoro, and other students also experienced difficulties getting back to their homes. Sarah had the worst experience because she had to travel all the way to Vietnam. After fulfilling the many requirements for travel, she was still unable to go because the fare was so expensive. Her trip would first require a flight from Manila to Japan. From there she would fly to Cambodia. Then, she would travel by bus to Hoh Chi Minh City. The cost would be about 200,000 pesos. In the end, she had to stay here with us alone for nearly a year.

Rather than just sit around waiting, Sarah decided to enroll in an online English language course. This all turned out to be a blessing in disguise. After taking this course, her English was greatly improved, and she could even be a translator for English-speaking ministers visiting Vietnam.

37

My Premonitions

Remember the thoughts I had involving the 13th batch due to the unpleasantness of the number? The pandemic came, whether we liked it or not, and the premonition I had about that batch proved true. Graduation that year was to be in November, but the schedule was disrupted. This also required that the opening of the 14th batch course had to be delayed. For the first time in many years, our graduation had to be postponed. Ultimately, it was conducted online. Eventually Sarah was able to find more affordable travel and returned to Vietnam.

The Pandemic also presented me with a totally new experience. Since all of our weekly services had to be held online, I had to prepare, not only my messages, but also some corresponding PowerPoint presentations. I had never done this before, and it taught me to do more expository preaching. I took my messages from many of the New Testament books, like Philippians 1st and 2nd Thessalonians, 1st and 2nd Timothy, Titus, James, 1st and 2nd Peter, 1st, 2nd and 3rd John, and Jude. I also did some expository preaching of the first chapters in Psalms, some chapters in Ecclesiastes, and also Romans and Hebrews. It was a great learning experience for me.

For the first time, with the 13th batch, we had scheduled a missions trip. Tickets had already been purchased, and activities had been planned in Vietnam, Cambodia, and Thailand.

We had taken an advance trip in April of 2019, and our goal was to prepare the way for an eventual trip for those soon to graduate in the 13th batch. Every student had gotten a passport and was preparing to leave the country. Until this time, all of the required mission trips for the students were taken inside the country. Such a mission trip was a requirement for graduation, and this had been true from the very first batch. On these trips, prospective graduates would minister in churches, to local students, and in any other open doors. Every part of these programs would be performed by students—song leading, testifying, praying, and delivering a message. A team leader would assign each one to do something, and they were all expected to carry it out with the Lord's help.

Because of this great responsibility, the students observed required days of prayer and fasting, and spiritual preparation for these events was a must.

My Premonitions

The costs for all of this travel were enormous, but God provided in many different ways. He especially used our Taiwanese brothers. This program was part of the vision of Paz from the first batch. Every month since then, whether far or near, we had worked to teach these students to trust God for His leading and His provision. He would have to provide open doors for the ministry and do what was necessary to promote the school.

From the beginning, we had a steady enrollment coming from different parts of the Philippines. We had prayed that somehow in the future God would grant us the opportunity, not only to do the mission trips inside the Philippines, but also in other countries, and are trusting God for more youth to come from the neighboring countries, such as Vietnam, Cambodia, and Thailand.

Paz and I are getting older, and sometimes our bodies don't seem to cooperate, but our vision for the Lord's work has not dimmed, and we look forward to the future. Serving God is such a great joy!

— Messages —

Allow me to share, in the pages to come, a few of the messages the Lord has given me in recent years.

—*Bert Colosaga*

THE LORD IS MY SHEPHERD

One of the many churches we visited on our tour of Jerusalem was the Church of All Nations in the Garden of Gethsemane. On one wall in that garden the Lord's Prayer was engraved in many languages. There was a version in Tagalog. There was also Spanish, French, German, Italian, and Portuguese, and, of course, there was English. Through my Bible studies, I learned that the Lord's Prayer can also be found in Psalm 23.

This psalm, very familiar to most of us, was sung by David, himself a shepherd, portraying the Lord as our Great Shepherd. *"The Lord is my Shepherd,"* he said in the first verse. I would like to put forward the following points about the Lord's Prayer in Psalm 23.

Our Father is the Great Shepherd. Psalm 80:1 says of Him:

Open your ears, O Roeh of Israel,
 the one who leads the descendants of Joseph like sheep,

the one who is enthroned over the angels.
(NOG)

The New International Version renders this verse:

Hear us, Shepherd of Israel,
  you who lead Joseph like a flock.
You who sit enthroned between the cherubim,
shine forth.

We also read about the Lord Jesus being our Shepherd in the New Testament. Jesus Himself said in John 11:1:

"I am the good shepherd. The good shepherd lays down his life for the sheep."

In verses 14-15, He said:

"I am the good shepherd; I know my sheep and my sheep know me—just as the Father knows me and I know the Father—and I lay down my life for the sheep."

There was an instance in which Jesus addressed Peter in this way:

Like a Dream

> *When they had finished eating, Jesus said to Simon Peter, "Simon son of John, do you love me more than these?"*
>
> *"Yes, Lord," he said, "you know that I love you."*
>
> *Jesus said, "Feed my lambs."*
>
> *Again Jesus said, "Simon son of John, do you love me?"*
>
> *He answered, "Yes, Lord, you know that I love you."*
>
> *Jesus said, "Take care of my sheep."*
>
> *The third time he said to him, "Simon son of John, do you love me?"*
>
> *Peter was hurt because Jesus asked him the third time, "Do you love me?" He said, "Lord, you know all things; you know that I love you."*
>
> *Jesus said, "Feed my sheep."* John 21:15-17, NIV

The Great Shepherd has called us to shepherd others.

Again we are speaking about the Lord's Prayer. *"Our Father who art in heaven"* is stating generally where God was and where God is.

"Hallowed be your name." God has many names.

"Your Kingdom come, your will be done, on earth as it is in heaven." What is Heaven like? Revelation 21:3-4 declares:

The Lord Is My Shepherd

And I heard a loud voice from the throne saying, "Look! God's dwelling place is now among the people, and he will dwell with them. They will be his people, and God himself will be with them and be their God. 'He will wipe every tear from their eyes. There will be no more death' or mourning or crying or pain, for the old order of things has passed away."

"I shall not want." Psalm 23 speaks about the Lord being our El-Shaddai, our Provider and Waymaker. This Hebrew name, El Shaddai, speaks of the God who is more than enough. He is our Supplier. It appears only eight times in the Old Testament and means the Almighty, all-sufficient God. Sometimes the name is shortened to Shaddai. Yes, I agree with David, I shall not want because El Shaddai is my Shepherd.

In verse 2-3, the 23rd Psalm declares:

He makes me lie down in green pastures,
he leads me beside quiet waters,
   he refreshes my soul.

Like a Dream

What does it mean to lie down in green pastures? It means rest. What does it mean to be led beside quiet waters? It means refreshing.

In Matthew 6:11, Jesus taught us to pray:

Give us today our daily bread.

When we lie down in green pastures and are led beside still waters, our daily needs are being provided.

Paul wrote:

Not that I desire your gifts; what I desire is that more be credited to your account. I have received full payment and have more than enough. I am amply supplied, now that I have received from Epaphroditus the gifts you sent. They are a fragrant offering, an acceptable sacrifice, pleasing to God. And my God will meet all your needs according to the riches of his glory in Christ Jesus. Philippians 4:17-19

The Lord-Sabaoth is with us. He is "the Lord who helps us." Yes, our Lord will help us to be overcomers. The name Jehovah-Sabaoth means "Lord of Hosts, the God of battles, and is used 282 times in the Bible. It is actually a military

The Lord Is My Shepherd

term. The "hosts" were the armies, and our God is the Lord of those hosts. David knew Johavah-Saboath:

> *Then said David to the Philistine, Thou comest to me with a sword, and with a spear, and with a shield: but I come to thee in the name of the LORD of hosts, the God of the armies of Israel, whom thou hast defied. This day will the LORD deliver thee into mine hand; and I will smite thee, and take thine head from thee; and I will give the carcases of the host of the Philistines this day unto the fowls of the air, and to the wild beasts of the earth; that all the earth may know that there is a God in Israel. And all this assembly shall know that the LORD saveth not with sword and spear: for the battle is the LORD's, and he will give you into our hands.* 1 Samuel 17:45-47, KJV

> *O Elohim Tsebaoth, restore us and smile on us so that we may be saved.* Psalm 80:7, NOG
> *Even though I walk through the dark valley of death,*
> *because you are with me, I fear no harm.*
> *Your rod and your staff give me courage.*
> Psalm 23:4, NOG

Like a Dream

There will be times of danger in our journey, but God is with us during our times of crisis. He has promised to see us through. As Jesus taught, our prayer should be:

Do not bring us into hard testing, but keep us safe from the Evil One. Matthew 6:13, GNT

The New International Version says it this way:

And lead us not into temptation,
 but deliver us from the evil one.

In Psalm 23:4 David said:

Yea, though I walk through the valley of the shadow of death, I will fear no evil: for thou art with me; thy rod and thy staff they comfort me. (KJV)

Jesus said to His disciples:

A time is coming and in fact has come when you will be scattered, each to your own home. You will leave me all alone. Yet I am not alone, for my Father is with me. I have told you these

The Lord Is My Shepherd

things, so that in me you may have peace. In this world you will have trouble. But take heart! I have overcome the world.

John 16:32-33, NIV

John also recorded:

You, dear children, are from God and have overcome them, because the one who is in you is greater than the one who is in the world.

1 John 4:4, NIV

Our God is our Savior, our Redeemer, and our Forgiver:

And forgive us our sins just as we have forgiven those who have sinned against us. ... Your heavenly Father will forgive you if you forgive those who sin against you; but if you refuse to forgive them, he will not forgive you.

Matthew 6:12 and 14-15, TLB

I am a failure, but He is my God. I am a sinner, but He is my Savior. I am broken, but He is my Healer. I am His child, and He is my God. Psalm 23:3 in the English Standard Version says:

He restores my soul.
He leads me in paths of righteousness
  for his name's sake.

The fact that He restores my soul shows that there is healing. The fact that He leads me in the paths of righteousness shows that there is guidance. He does it for His name's sake, and that is His purpose for each and every one of us.

Jesus was talking about His beloved disciples when He said:

Suppose one of you has a hundred sheep and loses one of them. Doesn't he leave the ninety-nine in the open country and go after the lost sheep until he finds it? And when he finds it, he joyfully puts it on his shoulders and goes home. Then he calls his friends and neighbors together and says, "Rejoice with me; I have found my lost sheep." I tell you that in the same way there will be more rejoicing in heaven over one sinner who repents than over ninety-nine righteous persons who do not need to repent. Luke 15:4-7, NIV

When a sheep becomes lost, even if it is because of willful disobedience, the Good Shepherd leaves the ninety-nine to find that lost one. Hebrews 9:12 declares:

He did not enter by means of the blood of goats and calves; but he entered the Most Holy Place once for all by his own blood, thus obtaining eternal redemption.

The last point I want to share is *Shalom*. Welcome to God's Kingdom. In Bible days, the word *shalom* was used as a familiar greeting, but it holds a deeper meaning for us. It was used by Jesus to describe His Kingdom and to speak to the very hopes and longings of the human heart. David said in his prayer:

You prepare a table before me
  in the presence of my enemies.
You anoint my head with oil;
  my cup overflows.   Psalm 23:5, NIV

Like a Dream

What was He saying? The Message translation says it this way:

> *You serve me a six-course dinner*
> *right in front of my enemies.*
> *You revive my drooping head;*
> *my cup brims with blessing.*

Matthew 6:13 concludes:

> *For thine is the kingdom, and the power, and the glory, for ever. Amen.*

David concluded his psalm:

> *Surely your goodness and love will follow me*
> *all the days of my life,*
> *and I will dwell in the house of the L*ORD
> *forever.* NIV

The Message translation says it this way:

> *Your beauty and love chase after me*
> *every day of my life.*

*I'm back home in the house of God
for the rest of my life.*

In New Testament times, Jesus was comforting His disciples when He said:

Do not let your hearts be troubled. You believe in God believe also in me. My Father's house has many rooms; if that were not so, would I have told you that I am going there to prepare a place for you? And if I go and prepare a place for you, I will come back and take you to be with me that you also may be where I am. John 14:1-3

Oh, praise the Lord!

The Gospel According to Isaiah 53

"Who would have believed what we now report?"

Who could have seen the LORD's hand in this?
Verse 1, GNT

1. Who would believe the Good News of the Gospel of Jesus Christ?
A. The Lord's hand in all of this:

*It was the will of the LORD that his servant
grow like a plant taking root in dry ground.*
Verse 2a

2. Jesus was born and grew in humility:

*He had no dignity or beauty
to make us take notice of him.
There was nothing attractive about him,
nothing that would draw us to him.* Verse 2b

2. For God so loved the world (John 3:16).

God loved, and for love, He allowed Jesus:

A. To be despised, rejected, and ignored.

We despised him and rejected him;
  he endured suffering and pain.
No one would even look at him—
  we ignored him as if he were nothing.
                                              Verse 3

B. It was for love that He endured suffering and pain in our place. Verse 4 says:

But he endured the suffering that should have been ours,
  the pain that we should have borne.
All the while we thought that his suffering
  was punishment sent by God.   Verse 4

3. For love, He was wounded, beaten, and suffered loss for us:

Like a Dream

> *But because of our sins he was wounded,*
> *   beaten because of the evil we did.*
> *We are healed by the punishment he suffered,*
> *   made whole by the blows he received.*
>
> Verse 5

4. For love, God gave His only Son:

> *For God so loved the world that He gave His only Son.*   John 3:16

He gave His only Son, and Jesus became our substitute, which is written in verse 6 of Isaiah 53:

> *All of us were like sheep that were lost,*
> *   each of us going his own way.*
> *But the* LORD *made the punishment fall on him,*
> *   the punishment all of us deserved.*   Verse 6

He gave His only Son, and Jesus, like a sheep, offered no resistance:

> *He was treated harshly, but endured it humbly;*
> *   he never said a word.*
> *Like a lamb about to be slaughtered,*

like a sheep about to be sheared,
he never said a word. Verse 7

Jesus died for our sins, crucified as a criminal:

He was arrested and sentenced and led off to die,
and no one cared about his fate.
He was put to death for the sins of our people.
Verse 8

Yes, Jesus died for our sins:

He was placed in a grave with those who are evil,
he was buried with the rich,
even though he had never committed a crime
or ever told a lie. Verse 9

Jesus' death was for our reconciliation with God:

1. His death was for forgiveness and eternal life.

The LORD says,
"It was my will that he should suffer;
his death was a sacrifice to bring forgiveness.

Like a Dream

And so he will see his descendants;
he will live a long life,
and through him my purpose will succeed.
Verse 10

2. Jesus' death was for everlasting joy and exultation among the redeemed:

After a life of suffering, he will again have joy;
he will know that he did not suffer in vain.
My devoted servant, with whom I am pleased,
will bear the punishment of many
and for his sake I will forgive them.
And so I will give him a place of honor,
a place among the great and powerful.
He willingly gave his life
and shared the fate of evil men.
He took the place of many sinners
and prayed that they might be forgiven.
Verses 11-12

4. Whosoever believes in Him will be saved:

For God so loved the world that He gave His only Son, that whosoever believes in Him ...

All of us were like sheep that were lost, each of us going his own way.

The people reply,
Who would have believed what we now report?
Who would have seen the LORD's hand in this?
                                  Good News Bible.

5. Who should not perish but have everlasting life:

Isaiah 53:12 says Jesus was a man delivered from the fate of evil. He willingly gave His life and shared the fate of evil men. He took the place of many sinners and prayed that they might be forgiven, that they might have everlasting life.

his death was a sacrifice to bring forgiveness.
And so he will see his descendants;
   he will live a long life,
   and through him my purpose will succeed.
                                           Verse 10

Praise God!

ESSENTIALS FOR GROWTH AND THE BUILDING UP OF THE BODY OF CHRIST

The Lord gave me a message on the essentials for growth and building up the Body of Christ. The texts I used were from Hebrews 10:1-18 and 22-39 and Ephesians 4:12-16. I originally entitled this message "Lettuce, Donuts, and Essentials to Growth in the Body of Christ."

Why did I use "lettuce"? Well, many of the verses I am referring to begin, *"Let us,"* and lettuce and other green leafy vegetables are known to be healthy foods. Some doctors and nutritionists even advise that it would be better for our health if we were vegetarians.

What about "donuts"? Donuts are categorized as a food to be taken in moderation, as they can cause heightened blood sugar. The Word of God often says, *"Do not,"* as we see in verses 35, 36, and 39 of Hebrews 10.

Hebrews 10:1-2 speaks about *"the shadow of real things to come."* Verses 3-4 show that the offerings of the Old

Essentials for Growth and the Building Up of the Body of Christ

Testament, even done repeatedly, could not take away sins. But Jesus Christ did away with the shadow and established the reality, and we know that as a fact.

Verse 7 declares that *"Jesus came and dwelt among us."*

Verses 8 and 12a show that when He came, He offered His body.

In verses 10 and 12b, He finished the task. As He hung on the cross, He offered some of His most powerful words: *"It is finished!"*

Verse 16 shows that He made covenant with us, putting His laws in our hearts and minds.

Verses 17-18 show that He forgot and forgave our sins.

So, what are the thirteen essentials for growth in the Body of Christ?

1. The Word of God tells us, *"Let us enter by a new and living way."* Jesus came and dwelt among us says John 1:14.

2. *"Let us draw near with a true heart in faith"* (Hebrews 10:22). To Know Him was our 2020 Grace Encounter theme. It was from John 17:3. Psalms 103:7 tells us that God revealed His plan to Moses and let the people of Israel know His mighty deeds.

3. *"Let us hold fast the conviction of our hope"* (Verse 23). To be like Christ, we need to say "HALO." HALO is our prototype in Christ to the Philippines, and it stands for Holiness, Accountability, Love, and Obedience.
4. *"Let us consider how to stir up one another to love and good works"* (Verse 24). We are to do what Jesus did. He said, *"As the Father sent me, so send I you"* (John 20:21b).
5. *"Do not neglect to meet together but encourage one another"* (Verse 25). To make Christ known, we are to fulfill the Great Commission found in Matthew 28:19: *"Therefore go and make disciples of all nations."*
6. *"Do not sin deliberately after receiving the knowledge of the truth"* (Verse 26).
7. *"Do not throw away your confidence, which has a great reward"* (Verse 35).
8. *"Do not shrink back, but instead you have faith"* (Verse 39). Here are all the requirements for the building up of the Body of Christ. *"The body is built up"* (Verse 12). The two words, *"so that,"* refer to the purpose behind serving—so that the body is built up.

Essentials for Growth and the Building Up of the Body of Christ

9. We will experience unity (see verse 13). The word *reach* here refers to travelers reaching their destination. Someone has said, "Disunity raises its ugly head when, on the sidelines, people talk about their own needs instead of serving sacrificially that the needs of others might be met."
10. We will have a renewed relationship with Christ (see verse 13). In a study called "Follow Me," an important factor in moving people to go deeper in their relationship with Jesus was that they serve regularly in some ministry.
11. We will have a mature membership (verse 11). In the last part of verse 13 and continuing in verse 14, we see that if we want to grow as a church, we must be involved in giving our time, talent, and treasures. If you want to grow, you must give out what you have been given.
12. We will experience spiritual stability. Spiritual stability comes when we are sold out in our service to God.
13. We will be linked in love (see verses 15-16). It is only as each part of the Body does its work that we will grow and be built up in love. In conclusion, the Lord needs servants, not superstars. He is looking for contributors, not consumers.

2 TIMOTHY 1
DISCIPLESHIP—PRINCIPLES
AND MOBILIZATIONS

1. A Generational Culture of Serving God: Vv. 3-5

A. Paul's Generation: *³ I thank God, whom I serve, as my ancestors did, with a clear conscience, as night and day I constantly remember you in my prayers. ⁴ recalling your tears, I long to see you, so that I may be filled with joy.*

B. Timothy's Family Generation: *⁵ I am reminded of your sincere faith, which first lived in your grandmother Lois and in your mother Eunice and, I am persuaded, now lives in you also.*

C. Timothy Now in Training: *² To Timothy, my dear son:* *⁵ᵃ I am reminded of your sincere faith,* *⁵ᵇ I am persuaded, now lives in you also.*

2. Loyalty for Mentors and the Gospel: Vv. 6-14

A. Jesus Christ Being Obedient to the Father: Vv. 8-10 *⁸ By the power of God. ⁹ He has saved us and called us to a holy life—not because of anything we*

DISCIPLESHIP—PRINCIPLES AND MOBILIZATIONS

have done but because of his own purpose and grace. This grace was given us in Christ Jesus before the beginning of time, ^{10} but it has now been revealed through the appearing of our Savior, Christ Jesus, who has destroyed death and has brought life and immortality to light through the gospel.

B. Paul, the Apostle, Obedient to Christ: *^{11} And of this gospel I was appointed a herald and an apostle and a teacher. ^{12} That is why I am suffering as I am. Yet this is no cause for shame, because I know whom I have believed, and am convinced that he is able to guard what I have entrusted to him until that day.*

herald, noun

1. an official messenger bringing news.
2. a person or thing viewed as a sign that something is about to happen. "They considered the first primroses as the herald of spring"

C. Timothy the Disciple, Fidelity to the Apostle Paul
^{6} For this reason I remind you to fan into flame the gift of God, which is in you through the laying on of my hands. ^{7} For the Spirit God gave us does not make us timid, but gives us power, love and self-discipline.

⁸ So do not be ashamed of the testimony about our Lord or of me his prisoner. Rather, join with me in suffering for the gospel, by the power of God.

D. Allegiance to the Gospel of Christ: *¹³ What you heard from me, keep as the pattern of sound teaching, with faith and love in Christ Jesus. ¹⁴ Guard the good deposit that was entrusted to you—guard it with the help of the Holy Spirit who lives in us.*

3. Examples of Disloyalty and Loyalty: Vv. 15-18

A. Disloyal to Their Calling: *¹⁵ You know that everyone in the province of Asia has deserted me, including Phygelus and Hermogenes.*

B. Loyal to the Very End: *¹⁶ May the Lord show mercy to the household of Onesiphorus, because he often refreshed me and was not ashamed of my chains. ¹⁷ On the contrary, when he was in Rome, he searched hard for me until he found me. ¹⁸ May the Lord grant that he will find mercy from the Lord on that day! You know very well in how many ways he helped me in Ephesus.*

2 TIMOTHY 2
DISCIPLE MAKERS—
CHARACTERISTICS

1. BE STRONG IN THE GRACE THAT IS IN CHRIST JESUS: Vv. 1-7

A. Continuity in the Calling for Service: V. 2 *² And the things you have heard me say in the presence of many witnesses entrust to reliable people who will also be qualified to teach others.*

B. Endurance of a Soldier: V. 3-4 *³ Join with me in suffering, like a good soldier of Christ Jesus. No one serving as a soldier gets entangled in civilian affairs, but rather tries to please his commanding officer.*

C. Stamina of an Athelete. V. 5 *⁵ Similarly, anyone who competes as an athlete does not receive the victor's crown except by competing according to the rules.*

D. Fortitude of a Farmer: V. 6 *⁶ The hardworking farmer should be the first to receive a share of the crops. ⁷ Reflect on what I am saying, for the Lord will give you insight into all this.*

2. BE PERSISTENT IN SUFFERING FOR CHRIST: Vv. 8-13

A. Jesus Christ, Raise from the Dead: V. 8 *8 Remember Jesus Christ, raised from the dead, descended from David.*

B. The Apostle Paul Chained Like a Criminal: Vv. 9-10 *9 for which I am suffering even to the point of being chained like a criminal. But God's word is not chained. 10 Therefore I endure everything for the sake of the elect, that they too may obtain the salvation that is in Christ Jesus, with eternal glory.*

C. Admonition to Believers: Vv. 11-13 *11 Here is a trustworthy saying: If we died with him, we will also live with him; 12 if we endure, we will also reign with him. If we disown him, he will also disown us; if we are faithless, he remains faithful, for he cannot disown himself.*

3. BE WISE IN DEALING WITH FALSE TEACHERS: Vv. 14-19

A. Keep reminding God's people: V. 14 *14 Keep reminding God's people of these things. Warn them before God against quarreling about words; it is of no value, and only ruins those who listen.*

DISCIPLE MAKERS—CHARACTERISTICS

B. Present Yourself to God as One Approved: V. 15 *15 Do your best to present yourself to God as one approved, a worker who does not need to be ashamed and who correctly handles the word of truth.*

C. Steer Clear of Foolish Discussions: V.16 *16 Avoid godless chatter, because those who indulge in it will become more and more ungodly.*

D. Description of False Teachers and Teachings: Vv. 17-18 *17 Their teaching will spread like gangrene. Among them are Hymenaeus and Philetus, 18 who have departed from the truth. They say that the resurrection has already taken place, and they destroy the faith of some.*

E. God's Truth Stands Firm: V. 19 *19 But God's truth stands firm like a great rock, and nothing can shake it. It is a foundation stone with these words written on it: "The Lord knows those who are really his," and "A person who calls himself a Christian should not be doing things that are wrong."*

4. BE STEADFAST AS GOD'S INSTRUMENTS FOR SPECIAL PURPOSE: Vv. 20-26

A. Special Purpose vs Common Use: Vv. 20-21 *20 In a large house there are articles not only of gold and silver, but also of wood and clay; some are for special*

> *purposes and some for common use. ²¹ Those who cleanse themselves from the latter will be instruments for special purposes, made holy, useful to the Master and prepared to do any good work.*

B. What to Do to Be God's Special Instrument: V. 22-23
   a. *Flee the evil desires of youth.*
   b. *Follow righteousness, faith, love and peace.*
   c. *Avoid foolish argument.*

C. Opponents Being Led to the Truth: V. 25-26
   > *²⁵ Adversaries must be gently instructed, in the hope that God will grant them repentance leading them to a knowledge of the truth, ²⁶ and that they will come to their senses and escape from the trap of the devil, who has taken them captive to do his will.*

2 TIMOTHY 3 DISCIPLESHIP— SUSTAINABILITY AMIDST CRISES

1. Godlessness in the Last Days: Vv. 1-4

A. Difficult times during these Last Days: Vv. 1-4

¹ But understand this, that in the last days there will come times of difficulty. ² For people will be lovers of self, lovers of money, proud, arrogant, abusive, disobedient to their parents, ungrateful, unholy, ³ heartless, unappeasable, slanderous, without self-control, brutal, not loving good, ⁴ treacherous, reckless, swollen with conceit, lovers of pleasure rather than lovers of God.

A Description of Godlessness: Lovers of self, lovers of money, lovers of the bad, lovers of pleasure, ungrateful, unholy, unappeasable, uncontrollable, slanderous, swollen with conceit, arrogant, abusive, proud, disobedient to parents, brutal, treacherous, reckless

A Description of the Godly: Loving God, loving neighbors.

2. The Deceitfulness of Ungodly People: Vv. 5-9

A. Wolves in Sheep clothing: Vv. 5-7 *⁵ having the appearance of godliness, but denying its power. Avoid such people. ⁶ For among them are those who creep into households and capture weak women, burdened with sins and led astray by various passions, ⁷ always learning and never able to arrive at a knowledge of the truth.*

B. Moses Being Opposed by Such People: Vv. 8-9 *⁸ Just as Jannes and Jambres opposed Moses, so these men also oppose the truth, men corrupted in mind and disqualified regarding the faith. ⁹ But they will not get very far, for their folly will be plain to all, as was that of those two men.*

3. Truthfulness Must Be Prevalent in Our Life and Teaching: Vv. 10-13

A. A Trainee Must Follow the Example of the Trainer: *¹⁰ You, however, have followed my teaching, my conduct, my aim in life, my faith, my patience, my love, my steadfastness, ¹¹ my persecutions and sufferings that happened to me at Antioch, at Iconium, and at Lystra—which persecutions I endured; yet from them all the Lord rescued me.*

DISCIPLESHIP—SUSTAINABILITY AMIDST CRISES

B. Following the Truth May Mean Persecution: Vv. 12-13 *[12] Indeed, all who desire to live a godly life in Christ Jesus will be persecuted, [13] while evil people and impostors will go on from bad to worse, deceiving and being deceived.*

4. Steadfastness, Look Back to the Basics: Vv. 14-17

A. Looking Back to Where You Were Hewn: Vv. 14-15 *[14] But as for you, continue in what you have learned and have firmly believed, knowing from whom you learned it [15] and how from childhood you have been acquainted with the sacred writings, which are able to make you wise for salvation through faith in Christ Jesus.*

B. Our Foundation Is Truly the Word of God: Vv. 16-17 *[16] All Scripture is breathed out by God and profitable for teaching, for reproof, for correction, and for training in righteousness, [17] that the man of God may be complete, equipped for every good work.*

2 TIMOTHY 4, DISCIPLESHIP— COMMISIONING AND LAUNCHING

1. Installation

¹ I charge you in the presence of God and of Christ Jesus, who is to judge the living and the dead, and by his appearing and his kingdom.

A. Job Descriptions, Steadfastness in Service: Vv. 2-5 *² preach the word; be ready in season and out of season; reprove, rebuke, and exhort, with complete patience and teaching. ⁵ᵇ Do the work of an evangelist, fulfill your ministry.* (TLB) *Bring others to Christ. Leave nothing undone that you ought to do.*

B. Last Days Compromising and Inconsistencies: Vv. 3-4 *³ For the time is coming when people will not endure sound teaching, but having itching ears they will accumulate for themselves teachers to suit their own passions, ⁴ and will turn away from listening to the truth and wander off into myths.*

2 TIMOTHY 4, DISCIPLESHIP—COMMISIONING AND LAUNCHING

2. Passing the Baton:

A. The Transfer of Responsibility: V. 6 *[6] For I am already being poured out as a drink offering, and the time of my departure has come.*

B. Starting Well, Finishing Even Better: V.7 *[7] I have fought the good fight, I have finished the race, I have kept the faith.*

C. The Reward for Paul's Faithfulness and also for Other Believers: V. 8 *[8] Henceforth there is laid up for me the crown of righteousness, which the Lord, the righteous judge, will award to me on that day, and not only to me but also to all who have loved his appearing.*

3. Final and Personal Exhortations:

A. People Who Deserted Paul: Vv. 10-16 *[10] for Demas has left me. He loved the good things of this life and went to Thessalonica. [14] Alexander the coppersmith has done me much harm. The Lord will punish him, [15] but be careful of him, for he fought against everything we said. [16] The first time I was brought before the judge, no one was here to help me. Everyone had run away. I hope that they will not be blamed for it.*

B. People who Supported Paul: Vv. 10-13 *[10] Crescens has gone to Galatia, Titus to Dalmatia. [11] Only Luke*

> *is with me. Bring Mark with you when you come, for I need him. ⁱ² (Tychicus is gone too, as I sent him to Ephesus.) ¹³ When you come, be sure to bring the coat I left at Troas with Brother Carpus, and also the books, but especially the parchments.*

C. The Lord Never Left Paul: Vv. 17-18 *¹⁷ But the Lord stood with me and gave me the opportunity to boldly preach a whole sermon for all the world to hear. And he saved me from being thrown to the lions. ¹⁸ Yes, and the Lord will always deliver me from all evil and will bring me into his heavenly Kingdom. To God be the glory forever and ever. Amen.*

JAMES 1
TRIED AND TESTED

"Life is a classroom in which each of us is being tested, tried, and passed."

1. What Does God Do When We Are Tried?

A. God Gives Perseverance Over Testing: Vv.2-4
² Consider it pure joy, my brothers and sisters, whenever you face trials of many kinds, ³ because you know that the testing of your faith produces perseverance. ⁴ Let perseverance finish its work so that you may be mature and complete, not lacking anything.

B. God Gives Wisdom Generously: V.5 *⁵ If any of you lacks wisdom, you should ask God, who gives generously to all without finding fault, and it will be given to you.*

C. God Strengthens Our Faith When We Are in Doubt: Vv. 6-8 *⁶ But when you ask, you must believe and not doubt, because the one who doubts is like a wave of the sea, blown and tossed by the wind. ⁷ That person should not expect to receive anything from the Lord. ⁸ Such a person is double-minded and unstable in all they do.*

2. What to Do When Trials Come:

A. Believers Must Stay Humble: V. 9 *⁹ Believers in humble circumstances ought to take pride in their high position.*

B. Believers Must Shun Pride Because It Brings Destruction: Vv. 10-11 *¹⁰ But the rich should take pride in their humiliation—since they will pass away like a wild flower. ¹¹ For the sun rises with scorching heat and withers the plant; its blossom falls and its beauty is destroyed. In the same way, the rich will fade away even while they go about their business.*

C. A Believer's Perseverance Assures a Crown: V. 12 *¹² Blessed is the one who perseveres under trial because, having stood the test, that person will receive the crown of life that the Lord has promised to those who love him.*

3. More Lessons on Trials

A. Temptations Originate from Man's Evil Desires: Vv. 13-16 *¹³ When tempted, no one should say, "God is tempting me." For God cannot be tempted by evil, nor does he tempt anyone; ¹⁴ but each per-*

son is tempted when they are dragged away by their own evil desire and enticed. ¹⁵ Then, after desire has conceived, it gives birth to sin; and sin, when it is full-grown, gives birth to death. ¹⁶ Don't be deceived, my dear brothers and sisters.

B. God Doesn't Tempt, but Gives Gifts: Vv. 17-18
¹⁷ Every good and perfect gift is from above, coming down from the Father of the heavenly lights, who does not change like shifting shadows. ¹⁸ He chose to give us birth through the word of truth, that we might be a kind of first fruits of all he created.

4. Lessons on Hearing and Obeying:

A. Be Quick to Listen, Slow to Speak and Avoid Anger: Vv. 19-21 *¹⁹ My dear brothers and sisters, take note of this: Everyone should be quick to listen, slow to speak and slow to become angry, ²⁰ because human anger does not produce the righteousness that God desires. ²¹ Therefore, get rid of all moral filth and the evil that is so prevalent and humbly accept the word planted in you, which can save you.*

B. After Hearing, It's Time to Obey: Vv. 22-25 *²² Do not merely listen to the word, and so deceive yourselves. Do what it says. ²³ Anyone who listens to the word but does not do what it says is like someone who looks at his face in a mirror* ^{24} *and, after looking at himself, goes away and immediately forgets what he looks like.* ^{25} *But whoever looks intently into the perfect law that gives freedom, and continues in it—not forgetting what they have heard, but doing it—they will be blessed in what they do.*

C. What Is True Religion? Vv. 26-27 ^{26} *Those who consider themselves religious and yet do not keep a tight rein on their tongues deceive themselves, and their religion is worthless.* ^{27} *Religion that God our Father accepts as pure and faultless is this: to look after orphans and widows in their distress and to keep oneself from being polluted by the world.*

JAMES 2
WHAT'S WRONG WITH DISCRIMINATION?

dis·crim·i·na·tion, noun

"The unjust or prejudicial treatment of different categories of people or things, especially on the grounds of race, age, or sex. (Victims of racial discrimination.)"

1. FAVORITISM FORBIDDEN:
A. **Avoid Discrimination:** Vv. 1-4 *[1] My brothers and sisters, believers in our glorious Lord Jesus Christ must not show favoritism. [2] Suppose a man comes into your meeting wearing a gold ring and fine clothes, and a poor man in filthy old clothes also comes in [3] If you show special attention to the man wearing fine clothes and say, "Here's a good seat for you," but say to the poor man, "You stand there" or "Sit on the floor by my feet," [4] have you not discriminated among yourselves and become judges with evil thoughts?*

B. **Deal Favorably with the Poor:** Vv. 5-7 *⁵ Listen, my dear brothers and sisters: Has not God chosen those who are poor in the eyes of the world to be rich in faith and to inherit the kingdom he promised those who love him? ⁶ But you have dishonored the poor. Is it not the rich who are exploiting you? Are they not the ones who are dragging you into court? ⁷ Are they not the ones who are blaspheming the noble name of him to whom you belong?*

C. **Follow the Royal Law of the Scriptures:** Vv. 8-10 *⁸ If you really keep the royal law found in Scripture, "Love your neighbor as yourself," you are doing right. ⁹ But if you show favoritism, you sin and are convicted by the law as lawbreakers. ¹⁰ For whoever keeps the whole law and yet stumbles at just one point is guilty of breaking all of it.*

D. **Watch What you Do and What you Think:** 12-13 (TLB) *¹² You will be judged on whether or not you are doing what Christ wants you to. So watch what you do and what you think; ¹³ for there will be no mercy to those who have shown no mercy. But if you have been merciful, then God's mercy toward you will win out over his judgment against you.*

2. FAITH AND WORKS:

What does James 2:26 mean by *"faith without works is dead?"* Here James affirms that deeds (or actions) are the by-product of a living faith.

A. **Faith and Deeds Explained:** Vv. 14-19 *[14] What good is it, my brothers and sisters, if someone claims to have faith but has no deeds? Can such faith save them? [15] Suppose a brother or a sister is without clothes and daily food. [16] If one of you says to them, "Go in peace; keep warm and well fed," but does nothing about their physical needs, what good is it? [17] In the same way, faith by itself, if it is not accompanied by action, is dead. [18] But someone will say, "You have faith; I have deeds." Show me your faith without deeds, and I will show you my faith by my deeds. [19] You believe that there is one God. Good! Even the demons believe that—and shudder.*

B. **Examples from the Bible**: Vv. 20-23
  1) Abraham: *[20] You foolish person, do you want evidence that faith without deeds is useless. [21] Was not our father Abraham considered righteous for what he did when he offered his son Isaac on the*

> *altar?* *²² You see that his faith and his actions were working together, and his faith was made complete by what he did. ²³ And the scripture was fulfilled that says, "Abraham believed God, and it was credited to him as righteousness," and he was called God's friend. ²⁴ You see that a person is considered righteous by what they do and not by faith alone.*

2) Rahab: *²⁵ In the same way, was not even Rahab the prostitute considered righteous for what she did when she gave lodging to the spies and sent them off in a different direction? ²⁶ As the body without the spirit is dead, so faith without deeds is dead.*

JAMES 3
TAMING THE TONGUE

"You can change your world by changing your words."

1. **Be Careful Little Tongue:** Vv. 1-2 *¹Dear brothers, don't be too eager to tell others their faults, for we all make many mistakes; and when we teachers of religion, who should know better, do wrong, our punishment will be greater than it would be for others.* (TLB)

   A. **Aiming for Perfection by Control of the Tongue:** Vv. 1-2 *¹ Not many of you should become teachers, my fellow believers, because you know that we who teach will be judged more strictly. ² We all stumble in many ways. Anyone who is never at fault in what they say is perfect, able to keep their whole body in check.*

   Proverbs 18:21 confirms this by saying, *"Death and life are in the power of the tongue, and those who love it will eat its fruits."*

Like a Dream

B. **Taming the Tongue Illustrated:** Vv. 3-8
   a) Horses: V. 3 *³ When we put bits into the mouths of horses to make them obey us, we can turn the whole animal.*
   b) Ships: V. 4 *⁴ Or take ships as an example. Although they are so large and are driven by strong winds, they are steered by a very small rudder wherever the pilot wants to go.*
   c) Forest Fire V. 5: *⁵ Consider what a great forest is set on fire by a small spark.*
   d) The Tongue V. 6: *⁶ The tongue also is a fire, a world of evil among the parts of the body. It corrupts the whole body, sets the whole course of one's life on fire, and is itself set on fire by hell.*
   f) Animals: Vv. 7-8 *⁷ All kinds of animals, birds, reptiles and sea creatures are being tamed and have been tamed by mankind, ⁸ but no human being can tame the tongue. It is a restless evil, full of deadly poison.*
C. **The Tongue Is to Praise God. Avoid Misusing It:** Vv. 9-12 *⁹ With the tongue we praise our Lord and Father, and with it we curse human beings, who have been made in God's likeness. ¹⁰ Out of the same mouth come praise and cursing. My brothers and sisters, this should not be. ¹¹ Can both fresh wa-*

ter and salt water flow from the same spring? [12] My brothers and sisters, can a fig tree bear olives, or a grapevine bear figs? Neither can a salt spring produce fresh water.

5 WAYS TO TAME YOUR TONGUE

Someone has suggested these five hints:

1. Dedicate your heart, mind, and tongue to the Lord daily.
2. Pray that God would give you an awareness/consciousness of your words.
3. Surrender your "right" to complain.
4. Ask for forgiveness for any unloving words or attitudes.
5. Practice speaking words that will encourage, comfort, edify, and inspire. [1]

Two Kinds of Wisdom

How is wisdom defined in the Bible?
1. Wisdom is an invaluable gift of God.
2. Wisdom is one of the most important virtues in life.

A. Earthly Wisdom: [13] *Who is wise and understanding among you? Let them show it by their good life, by*

1. Courtesy of Cornerstone Christian Counseling

> *deeds done in the humility that comes from wisdom. ¹⁴ But if you harbor bitter envy and selfish ambition in your hearts, do not boast about it or deny the truth. ¹⁵ Such "wisdom" does not come down from heaven but is earthly, unspiritual, demonic. ¹⁶ For where you have envy and selfish ambition, there you find disorder and every evil practice.*

B. Heavenly Wisdom: *¹⁷ But the wisdom that comes from heaven is first of all pure; then peace-loving, considerate, submissive, full of mercy and good fruit, impartial and sincere. ¹⁸ Peacemakers who sow in peace reap a harvest of righteousness.*

What is the difference between knowledge and wisdom? Knowledge is merely having clarity of facts and truths, while wisdom is the practical ability to make consistently good decisions in life.

JAMES 4
PRAYING OR PREYING
A Warning Against Greediness/Worldliness

¹ *What causes quarrels and what causes fights among you? Is it not this, that your passions are at war within you?*

Preying: "1. To make a raid for the sake of booty. 2. To seize and devour prey. 3. To commit violence or robbery or fraud."

1. A Warming Against Greediness—Fighting for Self:
Definition and Bible Verses about Greed: Greed goes much further than money. A person can be greedy for money but also for fame, possessions, attention, compliments, gifts, another person's time, and more. Greediness is always used to describe the selfish motivation of a person. Instead of being greedy, why not pray?

A. Reasons for Unanswered Prayers:
a) Covetousness: V. 2a *^{2a} You desire but do not have,*

so you kill. You covet but you cannot get what you want, so you quarrel and fight.

b) Failure to Ask: V. 2b *²ᵇ You do not have because you do not ask God.*

c) Wrong Motives: V. 3 *³ When you ask, you do not receive, because you ask with wrong motives, that you may spend what you get on your pleasures.*

d) Friendship with the World: V. 4 *⁴ You adulterous people, don't you know that friendship with the world means enmity against God? Therefore, anyone who chooses to be a friend of the world becomes an enemy of God.*

e) Pride: V. 6 *⁶ That is why Scripture says: "God opposes the proud.*

B. Reasons for Answered Prayers:

a) Submission: V. 7a *⁷ Submit yourselves, then, to God.*

b) Resisting the Devil: V. *⁷ᵇ Resist the devil, and he will flee from you.*

c) Coming Close to God: V. 8a *⁸ Come near to God and he will come near to you.*

d) Washing and Being Purified: V. 8b *⁸ Wash your hands, you sinners, and purify your hearts, you double-minded.*

e) In Tears, Cominh to the Lord: V. 9 *⁹ Grieve,*

mourn and wail. Change your laughter to mourning and your joy to gloom.

f) Being Humble: V. 10 *[10] Humble yourselves before the Lord, and he will lift you up.*

2. Watch and Pray: Vv. 11-12

   a) Guard Against Criticizing One Another: Vv. 11-12 *[11] Do not criticize one another, my friends. If you criticize or judge another Christian, you criticize and judge the Law. If you judge the Law, then you are no longer one who obeys the Law, but one who judges it. [12] God is the only lawgiver and judge. He alone can save and destroy. Who do you think you are, to judge someone else?* (GNB)

Watch and pray that you may not enter into temptation. The spirit indeed is willing, but the flesh is weak. Matthew 26:41

   b) Watch Against Boasting of Tomorrow (Take Life One Day at a Time): Vv. 13-16 *[13] Now listen to me, you that say, "Today or tomorrow we will travel to a certain city, where we will stay a year and go into business and make a lot of money." [14] You don't even know what your life tomorrow will be! You are like a puff of smoke, which appears for a moment and then disappears. ⁱ⁵ What you should say is this: "If the Lord is willing, we will live and do this or that." ¹⁶ But now you are proud, and you boast; all such boasting is wrong.*

Watch and pray that you may not enter into temptation. The spirit indeed is willing, but the flesh is weak. Mark 14:38

Do not boast about tomorrow, for you do not know what a day may bring. Proverbs 27:1

c) Watch About Knowing to Do Good and Not Doing It: V. 17 *¹⁷ So then, if we do not do the good we know we should do, we are guilty of sin.*

Continue steadfastly in prayer, being watchful in it with thanksgiving. Colossians 4:2

JAMES 5
WHAT ARE WE LIVING FOR?

1. **Do we Live for Prosperity and Prestige?** Vv. 1-6
   A. **Wealth is Temporary**: Vv. 1-5 *¹ Now listen, you rich people, weep and wail because of the misery that is coming on you. ² Your wealth has rotted, and moths have eaten your clothes. ³ Your gold and silver are corroded. Their corrosion will testify against you and eat your flesh like fire. You have hoarded wealth in the last days.*
   B. **Righteous Judgement Is Coming:** Vv. 4-6 *⁴ Look! The wages you failed to pay the workers who mowed your fields are crying out against you. The cries of the harvesters have reached the ears of the Lord Almighty. ⁵ You have lived on earth in luxury and self-indulgence. You have fattened yourselves in the day of slaughter. ⁶ You have condemned and murdered the innocent one, who was not opposing you.*

2. **Do We Live in Patience while Waiting/Suffering?** Vv. 7-12

Like a Dream

- A. Farmers Wait Patiently: Vv. 7-9 *⁷ Be patient, then, brothers and sisters, until the Lord's coming. See how the farmer waits for the land to yield its valuable crop, patiently waiting for the autumn and spring rains. ⁸ You too, be patient and stand firm, because the Lord's coming is near. ⁹ Don't grumble against one another, brothers and sisters, or you will be judged. The Judge is standing at the door!*
- B. The Examples of the Prophets: V. 10 *¹⁰ Brothers and sisters, as an example of patience in the face of suffering, take the prophets who spoke in the name of the Lord.*
- C. The Patience of Job: V. 11 *¹¹ As you know, we count as blessed those who have persevered. You have heard of Job's perseverance and have seen what the Lord finally brought about. The Lord is full of compassion and mercy.*
- D. Suffering and not Swearing: V. 12 *¹² Above all, my brothers and sisters, do not swear—not by heaven or by earth or by anything else. All you need to say is a simple "Yes" or "No." Otherwise you will be condemned.*

3. Do We Live Praying in Faith?
- A. Praying in Times of:

a) Trouble : V. 13 *¹³ Is anyone among you in trouble? Let them pray.*

b) Sickness: Vv. 14-15 *¹⁴ Is anyone among you sick? Let them call the elders of the church to pray over them and anoint them with oil in the name of the Lord. ¹⁵ And the prayer offered in faith will make the sick person well; the Lord will raise them up.*

c) Sin: Vv. 15-16 *¹⁵ If they have sinned, they will be forgiven. ¹⁶ Therefore confess your sins to each other and pray for each other so that you may be healed. The prayer of a righteous person is powerful and effective.*

d) Happiness: V. 13 *¹³ᵇ Let them sing songs of praise.*

B. Be Fervent in Prayer:

a) An Example in Fervency: Vv. 17-18 *¹⁷ Elijah was a human being, even as we are. He prayed earnestly that it would not rain, and it did not rain on the land for three and a half years. ¹⁸ Again he prayed, and the heavens gave rain, and the earth produced its crops.*

b) Praying for Backsliders: Vv. 19-20 *¹⁹ My brothers and sisters, if one of you should wander from the truth and someone should bring that person back,*

Like a Dream

[20] remember this: Whoever turns a sinner from the error of their way will save them from death and cover over a multitude of sins.

www.ingramcontent.com/pod-product-compliance
Lightning Source LLC
Chambersburg PA
CBHW032120090426
42743CB00007B/413